A.C.C.T.S. OF
PRAYER IN THE PSALMS

A*DORATION*

C*ONFESSION*

C*OMFORT*

T*HANKSGIVING*

S*UPPLICATION*

By Josiphine Longo

New King James Version
By Thomas Nelson Publishing

Compiled and written by Josiphine Longo

A.C.C.T.S. of Prayer in the Psalms
Copyright 2009©
Cover photo & design by Marshall Shepherd of Mars Photography &
Productions www.marsproductions.com

Published by:
Tididi Enterprises
PO Box 531223
St. Petersburg, FL 33747
www.tididi.com

ISBN
978-0-9815673-4-1
0-9815673-4-7

Please contact us for additional copies at: ministry@tididi.com or write to the address
above. Follow the blog: acctsofprayerinthepsalms.blogspot.com You can also purchase
books at the blog. (If mailing a check send $9.95 plus $2.95 s/h)

Proceeds support on going ministries and missions. For every book purchased at full
price we are able to give books away free. We work with churches, ministries and missions
to help get your books free of charge or to use as a fund raiser. Contact us at the email
above or go to the website for more information.

Table of Contents

Dedicated to my mother, Emma Longo, who prayed without ceasing for me all of my life. And to my son, Marshall Shepherd, whom, I shall never cease praying for, until the day the Lord comes again.

To my girlfriends Michele and Coralie who are my encouragement when I look at how the hand of the Lord changed their lives dramatically through prayer. And Deb who has always be there for me even if it is just to pray for me.

A special thanks to my mother, Emma, my sister Marian and my son Marshall who helped me with all the editing and layout of this book. I could never have done it all without there help.

❧ Introduction ❧

Prayer changes everything. Jesus promised in Matthew 7:7-8 *Ask, and it will be given to you; seek, and you will find' knock, and it will be opened to you. For everyone who asks receives, and he who seeks finds, and to him who knocks it will be opened.* The words pray/prayer were used 245 times in the Bible. It is our communication to heaven until we are face to face with our Lord. A.C.C.T.S., is an acronym for Adoration or Acknowledgement, Confession, Comfort, Thanksgiving (& Praise) and Supplication. It is a simplified format that we get from the Lord's prayer. (Matthew 6:9-13)

This book, *A.C.C.T.S. of Prayer in the Psalms*, is a result of my feeling distant from God and asking Him to help me know Him better and to learn to trust Him by knowing His character. He directed me to the Psalms, which was one book that I admit I had not spent enough time reading. I spent months reading and rereading the Psalms. Each time I read it with a new awareness and appreciation for the Lord.

I can see why God said David was a man after His own heart. David did not hold back his feelings and expressed all of them in the Psalms. How pure and honest he was with the Lord. I'm so thankful that he wrote down those feelings, expressing feelings and emotions that we all have, but may not know how to express them to the Lord.

The first time through the Psalms, I only looked for verses that gave me Gods character, but I kept seeing the other topics and so my quest began. I started with listing the words that described the Lord and His character. Wow, the comfort that I began to feel and the confidence of who He really is, has made my heart grow fonder for the Lord; especially for me, because I have found it difficult to trust anyone after being hurt by so many people in my life. So many times the topic I was searching, was where I was in life and the comfort of the Lord was there with me.

This has been a wonderful journey and I still love to read and reread the Psalms, highlighting those words that stand out to me when I am in need of the Lord's guidance. Each time I went through the Psalms I would see more things, like a topic jumps out, or a theme, or I would just receive the help and guidance I needed, at that very moment that I needed it. It is so good to know the Lord really is close with us, listening to us, hearing our hearts, our needs and our fears. It's easy to see that He really does care for each one of us individually.

The Lord loves to hear His word, so praying the scriptures is a sure way to get His attention. I have reworded a lot of these scriptures to be more of a conversation back to the Lord. For people learning to pray, I hope it will help to bring your heart closer to the Lord and you will see how close to you He really is. He really is a Man of His word.

Here is how A.C.C.T.S. is used following the Lord's Prayer format in the Psalms. (Matthew 6:9-13)

> **A** – ACKNOWLEDGE
> **C** – CONFESSION
> **C** – COMFORT
> **T** – THANKSGIVING
> **S** – SUPPLICATION

This was how Jesus teaching us to pray through the Lord's Prayer. The Lord's Prayer was not meant to be repeated like a mantra. But a format for us to follow.

It was also never meant to be said repetitively or as a mantra. The prayer was a demonstration of the principles of prayer. Let's look at it in depth. There are eight forms of: *adoration; confession, renewal, petition, intercession, affirmation, thanksgiving* and *closing prayer* are all illustrated in this model prayer.

Father in heaven, hallowed be Your name – The prayer principles of adoration (praise for who God is) and thanksgiving (praise for what He has done for me).

Your kingdom come; Your will be done on earth as it is in heaven – The principle of affirmation, that is, agreeing with God's will and submitting to it.

Give us today our daily bread – The principle of supplication, in which we make requests both for ourselves (petition) and for others (intercession).

And forgive us our debts as we also have forgiven our debtors – The principle of confession in view of our need for forgiveness of sins.

And lead us not into temptation, but deliver us from the evil one - The necessity of renewal as we face the temptations of the world, the flesh and the devil.

For Yours is the kingdom and the power and the glory forever – A closing prayer that honors the Lord and completes our thoughts.

Prayers of PETITION should be formatted around a 7-day cycle:
Monday - Growth in Christ
Tuesday - Growth in wisdom
Wednesday - Spiritual insight
Thursday - Relationships with others
Friday - Faithfulness as a steward
Saturday - Family and ministry
Sunday - Personal concerns

Prayers of INTERCESSION are also based on a weekly cycle:
Monday - Churches and ministries
Tuesday - Family
Wednesday - Believers
Thursday - Evangelism
Friday - Government
Saturday - Missions
Sunday - World affair

The format above can be found in Kenneth Boa's books "Face to Face, Praying the Scriptures for Intimate Worship." I recommend his books as they take you through 90 days of following the 7 step format of the Lord's Prayer: *Adoration, Confession, Renewal, Petition, Intercession, Affirmation, Thanksgiving* and closing prayer. He uses the entire bible so you will be studying the whole word as you pray the scriptures on a daily basis. Visit *www.kenboa.org*

Another format is by Daniel Henderson, which you can find on his website *www.strategicrenewal.com, The 29:59 Plan* is designed to equip you to spend 30 minutes a day in balanced, worship-based prayer (in a non-legalistic approach). This guide to communion with God is a comprehensive resource for a vital, Bible-based daily encounter with God and prayers that can change the world! He uses the prayer format *Upward - Downward - Inward - Outward.*

UPWARD IN REVERENCE, He is deserving of our praise.

DOWNWARD IN RESPONSE to surrender and yield.

INWARD IN REQUEST to seek His face for forgiveness and personal renewal.

OUTWARD IN READINESS with intercession for others, to get strength for the battle.

My goal and prayer for this book is to bring comfort for the hurting, direction for the lost, and healing for the heart through our Lord, Jesus Christ to anyone who would be willing to come.

Chapter 1

A.C.C.T.S.

WORDS THAT DESCRIBE GOD

Knowing the Lord and His character is the beginning of the relationship. Knowing the consistency of His character by the words that display and describe His character is the beginning of learning to trust in our creator, father, brother, husband and most important our eternal King.

ABUNDANT

36:8 They are abundantly satisfied with the fullness of Your house, and You give them drink from the river of Your pleasures.

86:5 For You, Lord, are good, and ready to forgive, and abundant in mercy to all those who call upon You.

86:15 But You, O Lord, are a God full of compassion, and gracious, longsuffering and abundant in mercy and truth.

130:7 O Israel, hope in the Lord; for with the Lord there is mercy, and with Him is abundant redemption.

ANSWERS

20:6 Now I know that the Lord saves His anointed; He will answer him from His holy heaven. With the saving strength of His right hand.

65:5 By awesome deeds in righteousness You will answer us, O God of our salvation, You who are the confidence of all the ends of the earth, and of the far-off seas.

91:15 He shall call upon Me, and I will answer him; I will be with him in trouble; I will deliver him and honor him.

99:8 You answered them, O Lord our God; You were to them God-Who-Forgives, Though You took vengeance on their deeds.

APPROACHABLE

65:4 Blessed is the man You choose, and cause to approach You, That he may dwell in Your courts. We shall be satisfied with the goodness of Your house, Of Your holy temple.

AWESOME

47:2 For the Lord Most High is awesome; He is a great King over all the earth.

65:5 By awesome deeds in righteousness You will answer us, O God of our salvation, You who are the confidence of all the ends of the earth, and of the far-off seas.

68:35 O God, You are more

awesome than Your holy places. The God of Israel is He who gives strength and power to His people. Blessed be God!

BEAUTIFUL

27:4 One thing I have desired of the Lord, That will I seek: That I may dwell in the house of the Lord all the days of my life, to behold the beauty of the Lord, and to inquire in His temple.

BLESSES

29:11 The Lord will give strength to His people; the Lord will bless His people with peace.

BOUNTIFUL

13:6 I will sing to the Lord, Because He has dealt bountifully with me.

68:19 Blessed be the Lord, Who daily loads us with benefits, the God of our salvation!

CLOTHED ME

30:11 You have turned for me my mourning into dancing; You have put off my sackcloth and clothed me with gladness.

COMPASSIONATE

78:38 But He, being full of compassion, forgave their iniquity, and did not destroy them.

111:4 He has made His wonderful works to be remembered; the Lord is gracious and full of compassion.

145:8 The Lord is gracious and full of compassion, slow to anger and great in mercy.

CONFIDENCE

65:5 By awesome deeds in righteousness You will answer us, O God of our salvation, You who are the confidence of all the ends of the earth, and of the far-off seas

COUNSELOR

33:11 The counsel of the Lord stands forever, the plans of His heart to all generations.

CREATOR

22:9 But You are He who took me out of the womb; You made me trust while on my mother's breasts.

33:6 By the word of the Lord the heavens were made, and all the host of them by the breath of His mouth.

33:9 For He spoke, and it was done; He commanded, and it stood fast.

71:6 By You I have been upheld from birth; You are He who took me out of my mother's womb.

100:3 Know that the Lord, He is God; it is He who has made us, and not we ourselves; we are His people and the sheep of His pasture.

119:73 Your hands have made me and fashioned me; give me understanding, that I may learn Your commandments.

119:90 Your faithfulness endures to all generations; You established the earth, and it abides.

DEEP

92:5 O Lord, how great are Your works! Your thoughts are very deep.

DEFENSE

59:9 I will wait for You, O You his Strength; for God is my defense.

59:16 But I will sing of Your power; yes, I will sing aloud of Your mercy in the morning; for You have been my defense and refuge in the day of my trouble.

62:2 He only is my rock and my salvation; He is my defense; I shall not be greatly moved.

62:6 He only is my rock and my salvation; He is my defense; I shall not be moved.

DELIGHTS IN ME

18:19 He also brought me out into a broad place; He delivered me because He delighted in me.

DELIVERER

18:2 The Lord is my rock and my fortress and my deliverer; my God, my strength, in whom I will trust; my shield and the horn of my salvation, my stronghold.

32:7 You are my hiding place; You shall preserve me from trouble; You shall surround me with songs of deliverance.

34:4 I sought the Lord, and He heard me, and delivered me from all my fears.

37:40 And the Lord shall help them and deliver them; He shall deliver them from the wicked, and save them, because they trust in Him.

40:17 But I am poor and needy; yet the Lord thinks upon me. You are my help and my deliverer; do not delay, O my God.

86:13 For great is Your mercy toward me, and You have delivered my soul from the depths of Sheol.

144:2 My lovingkindness and my fortress, My high tower and my deliverer, My shield and the One in whom I take refuge.

DWELLING PLACE

90:1 Lord, You have been our dwelling place in all generations.

ENLARGES MY PATH

18:36 You enlarged my path under me, so my feet did not slip.

EVERLASTING/FOREVER

10:16 The Lord is King forever and ever; the nations have perished out of His land.

45:6 Your throne, O God, is forever and ever; a scepter of righteousness is the scepter of Your kingdom.

48:14 For this is God, our God forever and ever; He will be our guide even to death.

66:7 He rules by His power forever; His eyes observe the nations.

72:17 His name shall endure forever; His name shall continue as long as the sun. And men shall be blessed in Him; all nations shall call Him blessed.

90:2 Before the mountains were brought forth, or ever You had formed the earth and the world, even from everlasting to everlasting, You are God.

93:2 Your throne is established from of old; You are from everlasting.

100:5 For the Lord is good; His mercy is everlasting, and His truth endures to all generations.

102:27 But You are the same, and Your years will have no end.

106:48 Blessed be the Lord God of Israel from everlasting to everlasting! And let all the people say, "Amen!" Praise the Lord!

119:152 Concerning Your testimonies, I have known of old that You have founded them forever.

119:160 The entirety of Your word is truth, and every one of Your righteous judgments endures forever.

134:3 The Lord who made heaven and earth. Bless you from Zion!

145:13 Your kingdom is an everlasting kingdom, and Your dominion endures throughout all generations.

146:10 The Lord shall reign forever - Your God, O Zion, to all generations. Praise the Lord!

EXALTED

47:9 The princes of the people have gathered together, the people of the God of Abraham. For the shields of the earth belong to God; He is greatly exalted.

EXCELLENT

76:4 You are more glorious and excellent than the mountains of prey.

FAITHFUL

36:5 Your mercy, O Lord, is in the heavens; Your faithfulness reaches to the clouds.

37:3 Trust in the Lord, and do good; dwell in the land, and feed on His faithfulness.

89:2 For I have said, "Mercy shall be built up forever; Your faithfulness You shall establish in the very heavens."

89:8 O Lord God of hosts, who is mighty like You, O Lord? Your faithfulness also surrounds You.

119:89 Forever, O Lord, Your word is settled in heaven.

FORGIVES

78:38 But He, being full of compassion, forgave their iniquity, and did not destroy them. Yes, many a time He turned His anger away, and did not stir up all His wrath.

86:5 For You, Lord, are good, and ready to forgive, and abundant in mercy to all those who call upon You.

99:8 You answered them, O Lord our God; You were to them God-Who-Forgives, though You took vengeance on their deeds.

103:3 Who forgives all your iniquities, who heals all your

diseases.

130:4 But there is forgiveness with You, that You may be feared.

FORTRESS

18:2 The Lord is my rock and my fortress and my deliverer; my God, my strength, in whom I will trust; my shield and the horn of my salvation, my stronghold.

31:2 Bow down Your ear to me, deliver me speedily; be my rock of refuge, a fortress of defense to save me.

31:3 For You are my rock and my fortress; therefore, for Your name's sake, lead me and guide me.

71:3 Be my strong refuge, to which I may resort continually; You have given the commandment to save me, for You are my rock and my fortress.

144:2 My lovingkindness and my fortress, my high tower and my deliverer, my shield and the One in whom I take refuge, who subdues my people under me.

GENTLE

18:35 You have also given me the shield of Your salvation; Your right hand has held me up, Your gentleness has made me great.

GLORY

8:1 O Lord, our Lord, How excellent is Your name in all the earth, who have set Your glory above the heavens!

19:1 The heavens declare the glory of God; and the firmament shows His handiwork.

64:10 The righteous shall be glad in the Lord, and trust in Him. And all the upright in heart shall glory.

72:19 And blessed be His glorious name forever! And let the whole earth be filled with His glory.

76:4 You are more glorious and excellent than the mountains of prey.

84:11 For the Lord God is a sun and shield; the Lord will give grace and glory; no good thing will He withhold from those who walk uprightly.

89:17 For You are the glory of their strength, and in Your favor our horn is exalted.

111:3 His work is honorable and glorious, and His righteousness endures forever.

145:5 I will meditate on the glorious splendor of Your majesty, and on Your wondrous works.

GOOD

33:5 He loves righteousness and justice; the earth is full of the goodness of the Lord.

86:5 For You, Lord, are good, and ready to forgive, and abundant in mercy to all those who call upon You.

100:5 For the Lord is good; His mercy is everlasting, and His truth endures to all generations.

106:1 Praise the Lord! Oh, give thanks to the Lord, for He is good!

107:1 Oh, give thanks to the Lord, for He is good! For His mercy endures forever.

118:1 Oh, give thanks to the Lord, for He is good! For His mercy endures forever.

GRACIOUS

84:11 For the Lord God is a sun and shield; the Lord will give grace and glory; no good thing will He withhold from those who walk uprightly.

103:8 The Lord is merciful and gracious, Slow to anger, and abounding in mercy.

116:5 Gracious is the Lord, and righteous; yes, our God is merciful.

145:8 The Lord is gracious and full of compassion, slow to anger and great in mercy.

GREAT

86:10 For You are great, and do wondrous things; You alone are God.

92:5 O Lord, how great are Your works! Your thoughts are very deep.

95:3 For the Lord is the great God, and the great King above all gods.

104:1 Bless the Lord, O my soul! O Lord my God, You are very great: You are clothed with honor and majesty,

GUIDES

25:9 The humble He guides in justice, and the humble He teaches His way.

32:8 I will instruct you and teach you in the way you should go; I will guide you with My eye.

73:24 You will guide me with Your counsel, and afterward receive me to glory.

HATES EVIL

97:10 You who love the Lord, hate evil! He preserves the souls of His saints; He delivers them out of the hand of the wicked.

HEALS

103:3 Who forgives all your iniquities, who heals all your diseases,

147:3 He heals the brokenhearted and binds up their wounds.

HEARS

10:17 Lord, You have heard the desire of the humble; You will prepare their heart; You will cause Your ear to hear,

17:6 I have called upon You, for You will hear me, O God; incline Your ear to me, and hear my speech.

18:6 In my distress I called upon the Lord, and cried out to my God; He heard my voice from His temple, and my cry came before Him, even to His ears.

34:4 I sought the Lord, and He heard me, and delivered me from all my fears.

34:15 The eyes of the Lord are on the righteous, and His ears are open to their cry.

65:2 O You who hear prayer, to You all flesh will come.

69:33 For the Lord hears the poor, and does not despise His prisoners.

106:44 Nevertheless He regarded their affliction, when He heard their cry.

145:19 He will fulfill the desire of those who fear Him; He also will hear their cry and save them.

Help/Helper

10:14 But You have seen, for You observe trouble and grief, to repay it by Your hand. The helpless commits himself to You; You are the helper of the fatherless.

30:10 Hear, O Lord, and have mercy on me; Lord, be my helper!

33:20 Our soul waits for the Lord; He is our help and our shield.

37:40 And the Lord shall help them and deliver them; He shall deliver them from the wicked, and save them, because they trust in Him.

46:1 God is our refuge and strength, a very present help in trouble.

54:4 Behold, God is my helper; the Lord is with those who uphold my life.

115:11 You who fear the Lord, trust in the Lord; He is their help and their shield.

Hides me/Hiding Place

27:5 For in the time of trouble He shall hide me in His pavilion; in the secret place of His tabernacle He shall hide me; He shall set me high upon a rock.

32:7 Rest in the Lord, and wait patiently for Him; do not fret because of him who prospers in his way, because of the man who brings wicked schemes to pass.

119:114 You are my hiding place and my shield; I hope in Your word.

Holds me up

18:35 You have also given me the shield of Your salvation; Your right hand has held me up, Your gentleness has made me great.

Holy

11:4 The Lord is in His holy temple, the Lord's throne is in heaven; His eyes behold, His eyelids test the sons of men.

15:1 Lord, who may abide in Your tabernacle? Who may dwell in Your holy hill?

20:6 Now I know that the Lord saves His anointed; He will answer him from His holy heaven with the saving strength of His right hand.

22:3 But You are holy, enthroned in the praises of Israel.

Honorable

111:3 His work is honorable and glorious, and His righteousness endures forever.

HOPE

16:9 Therefore my heart is glad, and my glory rejoices; my flesh also will rest in hope.

71:5 For You are my hope, O Lord GOD; You are my trust from my youth.

HOLY ONE

89:18 For our shield belongs to the Lord, and our king to the Holy One of Israel.

INHERITANCE

16:5 O Lord, You are the portion of my inheritance and my cup; You maintain my lot.

47:4 He will choose our inheritance for us, the excellence of Jacob whom He loves

106:5 That I may see the benefit of Your chosen ones, that I may rejoice in the gladness of Your nation, that I may glory with Your inheritance.

INSTRUCTS

94:12 Blessed is the man whom You instruct, O Lord, and teach out of Your law.

JOY

16:11 You will show me the path of life; in Your presence is fullness of joy; at Your right hand are pleasures forevermore.

JUDGE

9:8 He shall judge the world in righteousness, and He shall administer judgment for the peoples in uprightness.

98:9 Before the Lord, for He is coming to judge the earth. With righteousness He shall judge the world, and the peoples with equity.

JUST

33:4-5 For the word of the Lord is right, and all His work is done in truth. He loves righteousness and justice; the earth is full of the goodness of the Lord.

37:28 For the Lord loves justice, and does not forsake His saints; they are preserved forever, but the descendants of the wicked shall be cut off.

89:14 Righteousness and justice are the foundation of Your throne; mercy and truth go before Your face.

97:2 Clouds and darkness surround Him; righteousness and justice are the foundation of His throne.

103:6 The Lord executes righteousness and justice for all who are oppressed.

111:7 The works of His hands are verity and justice; all His precepts are sure.

KEEPS ME

66:9 Who keeps our soul among the living, and does not allow our feet to be moved.

121:5 The Lord is your keeper; the Lord is your shade at your right hand.

KIND/KINDNESS

31:21 Blessed be the Lord, for He has shown me His marvelous kindness in a strong city!

KING OF GLORY

24:7-10 Lift up your heads, O you gates! And be lifted up, you everlasting doors! And the King of glory shall come in. Who is this King of glory? The Lord strong and mighty, the Lord mighty in battle. Lift up your heads, O you gates! Lift up, you everlasting doors! And the King of glory shall come in. Who is this King of glory? The Lord of hosts, He is the King of glory.

47:2 For the Lord Most High is awesome; He is a great King over all the earth.

47:6 Sing praises to God, sing praises! Sing praises to our King, sing praises!

47:7 For God is the King of all the earth; Sing praises with understanding.

KNOWS MY THOUGHTS

94:11 The Lord knows the thoughts of man, that they are futile.

139:2 You know my sitting down and my rising up; You understand my thought afar off.

KNOWS THE HEART

33:15 He fashions their hearts individually; He considers all their works.

44:21 Would not God search this out? For He knows the secrets of the heart.

139:1 O Lord, You have searched me and known me.

LIFTS UP

3:3 But You, O Lord, are a shield for me, My glory and the One who lifts up my head.

4:6 There are many who say, "Who will show us any good?" Lord, lift up the light of Your countenance upon us.

18:48 He delivers me from my enemies. You also lift me up above those who rise against me; You have delivered me from the violent man.

30:1 I will extol You, O Lord, for You have lifted me up, and have not let my foes rejoice over me.

113:7 He raises the poor out of the dust, and lifts the needy out of the ash heap,

147:6 The Lord lifts up the humble; He casts the wicked down to the ground.

LIGHT

36:9 For with You is the fountain of life; in Your light we see light.

18:28 For You will light my lamp; the Lord my God will enlighten my darkness.

27:1 The Lord is my light and my salvation; whom shall I fear? The Lord is the strength of my life; of whom shall I be afraid?

97:4 His lightnings light the world; the earth sees and trembles.

119:105 Your word is a lamp to my feet and a light to my path.

119:130 The entrance of Your words gives light; it gives understanding to the simple.

LOOKING

53:2 God looks down from heaven upon the children of men, to see if there are any who understand, who seek God.

LORD OF HOSTS

24:10 WHO IS THIS KING OF GLORY? THE LORD OF HOSTS, HE IS THE KING OF GLORY.

LOVING

17:7 Show Your marvelous lovingkindness by Your right hand, O You who save those who trust in You from those who rise up against them.

25:6 Remember, O Lord, Your tender mercies and Your lovingkindnesses, for they are from of old.

26:3 For Your lovingkindness is before my eyes, and I have walked in Your truth.

36:7 How precious is Your lovingkindness, O God! Therefore the children of men put their trust under the shadow of Your wings.

36:10, Oh, continue Your lovingkindness to those who know You, and Your righteousness to the upright in heart.

42:8, The Lord will command His lovingkindness in the daytime, and in the night His song shall be with me— a prayer to the God of my life.

48:9 We have thought, O God, on Your lovingkindness, in the midst of Your temple.

63:3 Because Your lovingkindness is better than life, my lips shall praise You.

69:16 Hear me, O Lord, for Your lovingkindness is good; turn to me according to the multitude of Your tender mercies.

40:11 Do not withhold Your tender mercies from me, O Lord; let Your lovingkindness and Your truth continually preserve me.

103:4 Who redeems your life from destruction, who crowns you with lovingkindness and tender mercies.

MAJESTIC

29:4 The voice of the Lord is powerful; the voice of the Lord is full of majesty.

MEETS ME

59:10 My God of mercy shall come to meet me; God shall let me see my desire on my enemies.

MERCIFUL

21:7 For the king trusts in the Lord, and through the mercy of the Most High he shall not be moved.

25:6-7 Remember, O Lord,

Your tender mercies and Your lovingkindnesses, for they are from of old. Do not remember the sins of my youth, nor my transgressions; according to Your mercy remember me, for Your goodness' sake, O Lord.

32:10 Many sorrows shall be to the wicked; but he who trusts in the Lord, mercy shall surround him.

36:5 Your mercy, O Lord, is in the heavens; Your faithfulness reaches to the clouds.

62:12 Also to You, O Lord, belongs mercy; for You render to each one according to his work.

69:16 Hear me, O Lord, for Your lovingkindness is good; turn to me according to the multitude of Your tender mercies.

86:5 For You, Lord, are good, and ready to forgive, and abundant in mercy to all those who call upon You.

86:13 For great is Your mercy toward me, and You have delivered my soul from the depths of Sheol.

89:14 Righteousness and justice are the foundation of Your throne; mercy and truth go before Your face.

103:4 Who redeems your life from destruction, who crowns you with lovingkindness and tender mercies?

103:8 The Lord is merciful and gracious, slow to anger, and abounding in mercy.

103:11-12 For as the heavens are high above the earth, so great is His mercy toward those who fear Him; as far as the east is from the west, so far has He removed our transgressions from us.

103:17 But the mercy of the Lord is from everlasting to everlasting on those who fear Him,

106:1 Praise the Lord! Oh, give thanks to the Lord, for He is good! For His mercy endures forever.

108:4 For Your mercy is great above the heavens, and Your truth reaches to the clouds.

116:5 Gracious is the Lord, and righteous; yes, our God is merciful.

119:64 The earth, O Lord, is full of Your mercy; teach me Your statutes.

119:132 Look upon me and be merciful to me, as Your custom is toward those who love Your name.

119:156 Great are Your tender mercies, O Lord; revive me according to Your judgments.

MIGHTY

45:3 Gird Your sword upon Your thigh, O Mighty One, with Your glory and Your majesty.

89:8 O Lord God of hosts, who is mighty like You, O Lord? Your faithfulness also surrounds You.

MINDFUL

8:4 What is man that You are

mindful of him, and the son of man that You visit him?

111:5 He has given food to those who fear Him; He will ever be mindful of His covenant.

115:12 The Lord has been mindful of us; He will bless us.

144:3 Lord, what is man, that You take knowledge of him? Or the son of man, that You are mindful of him?

MOST HIGH

9:2 I will be glad and rejoice in You; I will sing praise to Your name, O Most High.

57:2 I will cry out to God Most High, to God who performs all things for me.

NEAR

34:18 The Lord is near to those who have a broken heart, and saves such as have a contrite spirit.

145:18 The Lord is near to all who call upon Him, to all who call upon Him in truth.

NEVER SLEEPS

121:4 Behold, He who keeps Israel shall neither slumber nor sleep.

PERFECT

18:30 As for God, His way is perfect; the word of the Lord is proven; He is a shield to all who trust in Him.

19:7 The law of the Lord is perfect, converting the soul; the testimony of the Lord is sure, making wise the simple.

WORDS THAT DESCRIBE GOD

POWERFUL

29:4 The voice of the Lord is powerful; the voice of the Lord is full of majesty.

66:7 He rules by His power forever; His eyes observe the nations; do not let the rebellious exalt themselves.

147:5 Great is our Lord, and mighty in power; His understanding is infinite.

PRESERVES

31:23 Oh, love the Lord, all you His saints! For the Lord preserves the faithful, and fully repays the proud person.

32:7 You are my hiding place; You shall preserve me from trouble; You shall surround me with songs of deliverance.

36:6 Your righteousness is like the great mountains; Your judgments are a great deep; O Lord, You preserve man and beast.

37:28 For the Lord loves justice, and does not forsake His saints; they are preserved forever, but the descendants of the wicked shall be cut off.

40:11 Do not withhold Your tender mercies from me, O Lord; let Your lovingkindness and Your truth continually preserve me.

97:10 You who love the Lord, hate evil! He preserves the souls of His saints; He delivers them out of the hand of the wicked.

145:20 The Lord preserves all who love Him, but all the wicked He will destroy.

PROVIDER

68:10 Your congregation dwelt in it; You, O God, provided from Your goodness for the poor.

PURE

12:6 The words of the Lord are pure words, like silver tried in a furnace of earth, purified seven times.

19:8 The statutes of the Lord are right, rejoicing the heart; the commandment of the Lord is pure, enlightening the eyes.

119:140 Your word is very pure; therefore Your servant loves it.

REDEEMERS

31:5 Into Your hand I commit my spirit; You have redeemed me, O Lord God of truth.

34:22 The Lord redeems the soul of His servants, and none of those who trust in Him shall be condemned.

55:18 He has redeemed my soul in peace from the battle that was against me, for there were many against me.

77:15 You have with Your arm redeemed Your people.

78:35 Then they remembered that God was their rock, and the Most High God their Redeemer.

REFUGE

9:9 The Lord also will be a refuge for the oppressed, a refuge in times of trouble.

14:6 You shame the counsel of the poor, but the Lord is his refuge.

46:1 God is our refuge and strength, a very present help in trouble.

46:7 The Lord of hosts is with us; the God of Jacob is our refuge.

46:11 The Lord of hosts is with us; the God of Jacob is our refuge.

59:16 But I will sing of Your power; yes, I will sing aloud of Your mercy in the morning; for You have been my defense and refuge in the day of my trouble.

62:7 In God is my salvation and my glory; the rock of my strength, and my refuge, is in God.

71:7 I have become as a wonder to many, but You are my strong refuge.

91:4 He shall cover you with His feathers, and under His wings you shall take refuge; His truth shall be your shield and buckler.

144:2 My lovingkindness and my fortress, my high tower and my deliverer, My shield and the One in whom I take refuge,

REMEMBERS

9:12 When He avenges blood, He remembers them; He does not forget the cry of the humble.

103:14 For He knows our frame; He remembers that we are dust.

105:8 He remembers His

covenant forever, the word which He commanded, for a thousand generations,

Reward

19:11 Moreover by them Your servant is warned, and in keeping them there is great reward.

Righteous

11:7 For the Lord is righteous, He loves righteousness; His countenance beholds the upright

36:6 Your righteousness is like the great mountains; Your judgments are a great deep; O Lord, You preserve man and beast.

36:10 Oh, continue Your lovingkindness to those who know You, and Your righteousness to the upright in heart.

71:24 My tongue also shall talk of Your righteousness all the day long.

89:14 Righteousness and justice are the foundation of Your throne; mercy and truth go before Your face.

89:16 In Your name they rejoice all day long, and in Your righteousness they are exalted.

97:6 The heavens declare His righteousness, and all the peoples see His glory.

103:6 The Lord executes righteousness and justice for all who are oppressed.

116:5 Gracious is the Lord, and righteous; yes, our God is merciful.

119:7 I will praise You with uprightness of heart, when I learn Your righteous judgments.

119:142 Your righteousness is an everlasting righteousness, and Your law is truth

145:17 The Lord is righteous in all His ways, gracious in all His works.

Rock

18:2 The Lord is my rock and my fortress and my deliverer; my God, my strength, in whom I will trust; my shield and the horn of my salvation, my stronghold.

18:31 For who is God, except the Lord? And who is a rock, except our God?

18:46 The Lord lives! Blessed be my Rock! Let the God of my salvation be exalted.

28:1 To You I will cry, O Lord my Rock: Do not be silent to me, lest, if You are silent to me, I become like those who go down to the pit.

31:3 For You are my rock and my fortress; therefore, for Your name's sake, lead me and guide me.

62:2 He only is my rock and my salvation; He is my defense; I shall not be greatly moved.

62:6 He only is my rock and my salvation; He is my defense; I shall not be moved.

62:7 In God is my salvation and my glory; the rock of my strength, and my refuge, is in God.

71:3 Be my strong refuge, to which I may resort continually; You have given the commandment to save me, for You are my rock and my fortress.

78:35 Then they remembered that God was their rock, and the Most High God their Redeemer.

92:15 To declare that the Lord is upright; He is my rock, and there is no unrighteousness in Him.

94:22 But the Lord has been my defense, and my God the rock of my refuge.

SAVES/SALVATION

37:40 And the Lord shall help them and deliver them; He shall deliver them from the wicked, and save them, because they trust in Him.

62:7 In God is my salvation and my glory; the rock of my strength, and my refuge, is in God.

65:5 By awesome deeds in righteousness You will answer us, O God of our salvation, You who are the confidence of all the ends of the earth, and of the far-off seas.

68:20 Our God is the God of salvation; and to GOD the Lord belong escapes from death.

91:16 With long life I will satisfy him, and show him My salvation."

SETS APART

4:3 But know that the Lord has set apart for Himself him who is godly; the Lord will hear when I call to Him.

SHADE

17:8 Keep me as the apple of Your eye; hide me under the shadow of Your wings,

121:5 The Lord is your keeper; the Lord is your shade at your right hand.

SHELTER

61:3 For You have been a shelter for me, a strong tower from the enemy.

SHEPHERD

23:1 The Lord is my shepherd; I shall not want.

80:1 Give ear, O Shepherd of Israel, You who lead Joseph like a flock; You who dwell between the cherubim, shine forth!

SHIELD

3:3 But You, O Lord, are a shield for me, my glory and the One who lifts up my head.

5:12 For You, O Lord, will bless the righteous; with favor You will surround him as with a shield.

18:2 The Lord is my rock and my fortress and my deliverer; my God, my strength, in whom I will trust; my shield and the horn of my salvation, my stronghold.

18:30 As for God, His way is perfect; the word of the Lord is proven; He is a shield to all who trust in Him.

18:35 You have also given me the shield of Your salvation; Your right hand has held me up, Your gentleness has made me great.

28:7 The Lord is my strength and my shield; my heart trusted in Him, and I am helped; Therefore my heart greatly rejoices, and with my song I will praise Him.

33:20 Our soul waits for the Lord; He is our help and our shield.

47:9 The princes of the people have gathered together, the people of the God of Abraham. For the shields of the earth belong to God; He is greatly exalted.

84:9 O God, behold our shield, and look upon the face of Your anointed.

84:11 For the Lord God is a sun and shield; the Lord will give grace and glory; no good thing will He withhold from those who walk uprightly.

89:18 For our shield belongs to the Lord, and our king to the Holy One of Israel.

115:11 You who fear the Lord, trust in the Lord; He is their help and their shield.

119:114 You are my hiding place and my shield; I hope in Your word.

144:2 My lovingkindness and my fortress, my high tower and my deliverer, my shield and the One in whom I take refuge.

WORDS THAT DESCRIBE GOD

SLOW TO ANGER

103:8 The Lord is merciful and gracious, slow to anger, and abounding in mercy.

145:8 The Lord is gracious and full of compassion, slow to anger and great in mercy.

STRENGTH

18:1 I will love You, O Lord, my strength.

18:2 The Lord is my rock and my fortress and my deliverer; my God, my strength, in whom I will trust; my shield and the horn of my salvation, my stronghold.

27:1 The Lord is my light and my salvation; whom shall I fear? The Lord is the strength of my life; of whom shall I be afraid?

27:14 Wait on the Lord; be of good courage, and He shall strengthen your heart; wait, I say, on the Lord!

28:7 The Lord is my strength and my shield; my heart trusted in Him, and I am helped; therefore my heart greatly rejoices, and with my song I will praise Him.

28:8 The Lord is their strength, and He is the saving refuge of His anointed.

29:11 The Lord will give strength to His people; the Lord will bless His people with peace.

31:24 Be of good courage, and He shall strengthen your heart, All you who hope in the Lord.

37:39 But the salvation of the righteous is from the Lord; He is their strength in the time of trouble.

46:1 God is our refuge and strength, a very present help in trouble.

59:17 To You, O my Strength, I will sing praises; for God is my defense, my God of mercy.

61:3 For You have been a shelter for me, a strong tower from the enemy.

62:7 In God is my salvation and my glory; the rock of my strength, and my refuge, is in God.

68:35 O God, You are more awesome than Your holy places. The God of Israel is He who gives strength and power to His people.

73:26 My flesh and my heart fail; but God is the strength of my heart and my portion forever.

77:14 You are the God who does wonders; You have declared Your strength among the peoples.

105:4 Seek the Lord and His strength; seek His face evermore!

STRONGHOLD/STRONG TOWER

18:2 The Lord is my rock and my fortress and my deliverer; my God, my strength, in whom I will trust; my shield and the horn of my salvation, my stronghold.

144:2 My lovingkindness and my fortress, my high tower and my deliverer, my shield and the One in whom I take refuge,

SUN

84:11 For the Lord God is a sun and shield; the Lord will give grace and glory; no good thing will He withhold from those who walk uprightly.

SUPPORT

18:18 They confronted me in the day of my calamity, but the Lord was my support.

SURE

19:7 The law of the Lord is perfect, converting the soul; the testimony of the Lord is sure, making wise the simple.

93:5 Your testimonies are very sure; holiness adorns Your house, O Lord, forever.

SUSTAINER OF LIFE

3:5 I lay down and slept; I awoke, for the Lord sustained me.

55:22 Cast your burden on the Lord, and He shall sustain you; He shall never permit the righteous to be moved.

TEACHER

25:8 Good and upright is the Lord; therefore He teaches sinners in the way.

25:12 Who is the man that fears the Lord? Him shall He teach in the way He chooses.

32:8 I will instruct you and teach you in the way you should go; I will guide you with My eye.

71:17 O God, You have taught me

from my youth; and to this day I declare Your wondrous works.

119:64 The earth, O Lord, is full of Your mercy; teach me Your statutes.

TENDER

25:6 Remember, O Lord, Your tender mercies and Your lovingkindnesses, for they are from of old.

103:4 Who redeems your life from destruction, who crowns you with lovingkindness and tender mercies.

TESTS THE RIGHTEOUS

7:9 Oh, let the wickedness of the wicked come to an end, but establish the just; for the righteous God tests the hearts and minds.

11:5 The Lord tests the righteous, but the wicked and the one who loves violence His soul hates.

THINKING OF ME

139:17 How precious also are Your thoughts to me, O God! How great is the sum of them!

THOUGHTFUL

40:5 Many, O Lord my God, are Your wonderful works which You have done; and Your thoughts toward us cannot be recounted to You in order; if I would declare and speak of them, they are more than can be numbered.

TO BE FEARED

19:9 The fear of the Lord is clean, enduring forever; the judgments of the Lord are true and righteous altogether.

25:14 The secret of the Lord is with those who fear Him, and He will show them His covenant.

76:7 You, Yourself, are to be feared; and who may stand in Your presence when once You are angry?

89:7 God is greatly to be feared in the assembly of the saints, and to be held in reverence by all those around Him.

96:4 For the Lord is great and greatly to be praised; He is to be feared above all gods.

130:3-4 If You, Lord, should mark iniquities, O Lord, who could stand? But there is forgiveness with You, that You may be feared.

147:11 The Lord takes pleasure in those who fear Him, in those who hope in His mercy.

TRUSTWORTHY

11:1 In the Lord I put my trust.

36:7 How precious is Your lovingkindness, O God! Therefore the children of men put their trust under the shadow of Your wings.

62:8 Trust in Him at all times, you people; pour out your heart before Him; God is a refuge for us.

64:10 The righteous shall be glad in the Lord, and trust in Him. And all the upright in heart shall glory.

71:5 For You are my hope, O Lord

GOD; You are my trust from my youth.

73:28 But it is good for me to draw near to God; I have put my trust in the Lord GOD, that I may declare all Your works.

118:8-9 It is better to trust in the Lord than to put confidence in man. It is better to trust in the Lord than to put confidence in princes.

TRUTH

19:9 The fear of the Lord is clean, enduring forever; the judgments of the Lord are true and righteous altogether.

33:4 For the word of the Lord is right, and all His work is done in truth.

40:11 Do not withhold Your tender mercies from me, O Lord; let Your lovingkindness and Your truth continually preserve me.

89:14 Righteousness and justice are the foundation of Your throne; mercy and truth go before Your face.

119:151-152 You are near, O Lord, and all Your commandments are truth. Concerning Your testimonies, I have known of old that You have founded them forever.

119:160 The entirety of Your word is truth, and every one of Your righteous judgments endures forever.

UPHOLDS

37:17 For the arms of the wicked shall be broken, but the Lord upholds the righteous.

37:24 Though he fall, he shall not be utterly cast down; for the Lord upholds him with His hand.

71:6 By You I have been upheld from birth; You are He who took me out of my mother's womb. My praise shall be continually of You.

UPRIGHT

25:8 Good and upright is the Lord; therefore He teaches sinners in the way.

WATCHES

33:13 The Lord looks from heaven; He sees all the sons of men.

33:18-19 Behold, the eye of the Lord is on those who fear Him, on those who hope in His mercy, To deliver their soul from death, and to keep them alive in famine.

66:7 He rules by His power forever; His eyes observe the nations; do not let the rebellious exalt themselves.

WILL NOT FORSAKE

9:10 And those who know Your name will put their trust in You; for You, Lord, have not forsaken those who seek You.

71:18 Now also when I am old and grayheaded, O God, do not forsake me, until I declare Your strength to this generation, Your power to everyone who is to come.

WISE

51:6 Behold, You desire truth in the inward parts, and in the hidden part You will make me to know wisdom.

104:24 O Lord, how manifold are Your works! In wisdom You have made them all. The earth is full of Your possessions.

111:10 The fear of the Lord is the beginning of wisdom; a good understanding have all those who do His commandments. His praise endures forever.

147:5 Great is our Lord, and mighty in power; His understanding is infinite.

WITH US

46:11 The Lord of hosts is with us; the God of Jacob is our refuge.

42:8 The Lord will command His lovingkindness in the daytime, and in the night His song shall be with me, a prayer to the God of my life.

WONDERFUL

40:5 Many, O Lord my God, are Your wonderful works which You have done; and Your thoughts toward us cannot be recounted to You in order; if I would declare and speak of them, they are more than can be numbered.

78:4 We will not hide them from their children, telling to the generation to come the praises of the Lord, and His strength and His wonderful works that He has done.

WORTHY

18:3 I will call upon the Lord, who is worthy to be praised; so shall I be saved from my enemies.

Chapter 2

3:3 But You, O Lord are a shield for me, my glory and the one who lifts up my head. I cried to You, Lord, with my voice and You heard me from Your holy hill.

3:5 I lay down and slept, I awoke, for You, Lord, sustained me.

3:8 Salvation belongs to You, Lord. Your blessing is upon me.

4:3 But I know that You, Lord, have set apart for Yourself those who are godly. Lord, You will hear when I call You.

4:6-8 Lord, lift up the light of Your countenance upon me. You have put gladness in my heart. I will both lie down in peace, and sleep. For You alone make me dwell in safety.

5:4 For You are not a God who takes pleasure in wickedness, nor shall evil dwell with You.

5:12 For You, O Lord, will bless the righteous; with favor You will surround me as with a shield.

7:9-10 For the righteous You, God, test our hearts and minds. My defense is of You, God, who saves the upright in heart.

8:1 O Lord, my Lord how excellent is Your name in all the earth. Who have set Your glory above the heavens.

8:3 When I consider Your heavens, the work of Your fingers, the moon, the stars, which you have ordained, what is man that You are mindful of me, and the son of man that you visit him? For you have made me a little lower than the angels, and you have crowned me with glory and honor.

9:10 We who know Your name will put our trust in You. For You, Lord, have not forsaken those who seek You.

10:14 The helpless commits himself to You. You are the helper of the fatherless.

10:17 Lord, You have heard the desire of the humble, You will prepare my heart, You will cause Your ear to hear me.

11:1 In You, Lord, I put my trust.

11:5 Lord, You test the righteous.

11:7 For You, Lord, are righteous. You love righteousness, Your countenance beholds the upright.

12:6 Your words, Lord, are pure like silver, tried in a furnace of earth, purified seven times.

13:6 I will sing to You, Lord, because You have dealt bountifully with me.

14:2 Lord, You look down from heaven upon the children of men, to see if there are any who understand, who seek You.

14:5 For You, God, are with the generation of the righteous.

15:1-3 Lord, who may abide in Your tabernacle? Who may dwell in Your holy hill? He who walks uprightly and works righteousness, and speaks the truth in his heart. He who does not backbite with his tongue, nor do evil to his neighbor, nor does he take up a reproach against his friend.

16:2 My goodness is nothing apart from You.

16:5 O Lord, You are the portion of my inheritance and my cup, You maintain my lot.

16:8 I have set You, Lord always before me; because You are at my right hand I shall not be moved.

17:6 I have called upon You and I know You will hear me, O God.

17:7 Show Your marvelous lovingkindness by Your right hand, O You, who save those who trust in You from those who rise up against them.

17:8 Keep me as the apple of Your eye and hide me under the shadow of Your wings from the wicked who oppress me, from my deadly enemies who surround me.

17:15 As for me, I will see Your face in righteousness; I shall be satisfied when I awake in Your likeness.

18:1-3 I will love You, O Lord, my strength. Lord, You are my rock and my fortress and my deliverer; God, You are my strength, in whom I will trust; my shield and the horn of my salvation, my stronghold. I will call upon You, Lord, who is worthy to be praised.

18:6 You heard my voice from Your temple and my cry came before You, even to Your ears.

18:18-19 But You, Lord, are my support. . . You delivered me because You delight in me.

18:28 For You will light my lamp. You, Lord, my God, will enlighten my darkness.

18:30 As for You God, Your way is perfect; Your word Lord is proven; You are a shield to all who trust in You.

18:31-33 For who is God, except You, Lord? And who is a rock, except You my God? It is You, God, who arms me with strength, and makes my way perfect. You make my feet like the feet of a deer, and set me on my high places.

18:35-36 You have also given me the shield of your salvation; Your right hand has held me up; Your gentleness has made me great. You enlarged my path under me, so my feet do not slip.

18:39 For You have armed me with strength for the battle.

18:46 Blessed be my rock! You, are the God of my salvation and I exalt You.

18:48 You also lift me up above those who rise against me.

19:1 The heavens declare the glory of You God; and the firmament shows Your handiwork.

19:7-11 Your law, Lord, is perfect, converting the soul; Your testimony, Lord, is sure, making wise the simple; Your statutes, Lord, are right, rejoicing my heart; Your commandment, Lord, is pure, enlightening the eyes; the fear of You, Lord, is clean, enduring forever; Your judgments, Lord, are true and righteous altogether. More to be desired are they than gold, Yea, than much fine gold; also than honey and the honeycomb. Moreover by them Your servant is warned, and in keeping them there is great reward.

20:6 Now I know that You, Lord, save Your anointed; You will answer me from Your holy heaven with the saving strength of Your right hand.

21:13 Be exalted, O Lord, in Your own strength! I will sing and praise Your power.

22.9 You are He who took me out of the womb.

23:1 Lord You are my shepherd, I shall not want.

24:8 Who is this King of glory, You, Lord, strong and mighty, You, Lord, mighty in battle. . . You are the King of Glory.

25:6 Remember O Lord, Your tender mercies and Your lovingkindness for they are from of old.

25:8-10 Good and upright are You, Lord, therefore You teach sinner in the way. The humble You guide in justice and the humble You teach You way. All You paths, Lord are mercy and truth.

25:12 Who am I that fears You, Lord? You shall teach me in the way You choose.

25:14 The SECRET of the Lord is with those who FEAR HIM and You will show me Your covenant.

26:3 For Your lovingkindness is before my eyes.

27:1 You are my light and my salvation, whom shall I fear? Lord, You are the strength of my life, of whom shall I be afraid?

27:4b-5 To behold the beauty of You, Lord, and to inquire in Your temple. For in the time of trouble You shall hide me in Your pavilion; in the secret place of Your tabernacle, You shall hide me; You shall set me high upon a rock.

27:8 When You said, "Seek My face," My heart said to you, "Your face, Lord, I will seek."

27:14 I will wait on You, Lord; I will be of good courage; and You shall strengthen my heart; I will wait, I say, on You, Lord!

28:7 Lord You are my strength and my shield; my heart trusts in You, and I am helped, therefore my heart greatly rejoices and with my song I will praise You.

28:8 Lord You are my strength and You are the saving refuge of Your anointed.

29:4 Your voice Lord, is powerful. Your voice Lord, is full of majesty.

29:11 Lord You will give strength to Your people. Lord you will bless Your people with peace.

30:1 I will extol you, O Lord, for you have lifted me up, and have not let my foes rejoice over me.

30:11 You have turned for me my mourning into dancing. You have put off my sackcloth and clothed me with gladness.

31:3 For you are my rock and my fortress.

31:5 Into Your hand I commit my spirit, You have redeemed me, O Lord, God of truth.

31:19 Oh how great is Your goodness, which You have laid up for those who fear You. Which You have prepared for those who trust You.

31:21 Blessed be the Lord, for You have shown me Your marvelous kindness. . .

31:23-24 Oh, I love You, Lord, I am one of your saints! For Lord You preserve the faithful. I shall be of good courage because You shall strengthen my heart. I put my hope in You, Lord.

32:7 You are my hiding place; You shall preserve me from trouble; You shall surround me with songs of deliverance.

32:8 You will instruct me and teach me in the way I should go.

You will guide me with Your eye.

32:10 Many sorrows shall be to the wicked; but I will put my trust in You, Lord, and mercy shall surround me.

33:4-5 For Your word Lord is right and all Your work is done in truth. You love righteousness and justice. The earth is full of Your goodness Lord.

33:6 By Your word Lord, the heavens were made, and all the host of them by the breath of Your mouth.

33:9 For You spoke and it was done; You commanded and it stood fast.

33:11 Your counsel Lord stands forever.

33:13, 15 Lord You look from heaven; You see all the sons of men. You fashion our hearts individually; You consider all my works.

33:18-20 Behold Your eye Lord is on those who fear You. On those who hope in Your mercy, to deliver our soul from death and to keep us alive in famine. My soul waits for You, Lord. You are my help and my shield.

34:4 I sought You, Lord, and You heard me and delivered me from all my fear.

34:10 But when I seek You, Lord, I shall not lack any good thing.

34:15 Your eyes Lord, are on the righteous, and Your ears are open to my cry.

34:18 Lord, You are near to me, I have a broken heart, and You save such as have a contrite spirit.

34:22 Lord, You redeem the soul of Your servants, and none of us who trust in You shall be condemned.

36:5-6 Your mercy O Lord, is in the heavens; Your faithfulness reaches to the clouds. Your righteousness is like the great mountains, Your judgments are a great deep; O Lord You preserve man and beast.

36:7-9 How precious is Your lovingkindness, O God! Therefore I put my trust under the shadow of Your wings. I will be abundantly satisfied with the fullness of Your house, and You give me drink from the river of Your pleasures. For with You is the fountain of life; in Your light I see light.

36:10 Oh, continue Your lovingkindness to those who know You, and Your righteousness to the upright in heart.

37:3 I will trust in You, Lord, and do good; dwell in the land, and feed on Your faithfulness.

37:17 Lord You uphold the righteous.

37:23-24 The steps of a good person are ordered by You, Lord, and You delight in my way. Though I fall, I shall not be utterly cast down; for You, Lord, uphold me with Your hand.

37:28 For You, Lord, love justice, and will not forsake Your saints; I am preserved forever.

37:39-40 But my salvation as one of the righteous is from You, Lord. You are my strength in time of trouble and Lord, You shall help me and deliver me; You shall deliver me from the wicked, and save me, because I trust in You.

40:5 Many, O Lord my God, are Your wonderful works, which You have done; and Your thoughts toward me cannot be recounted in order; if I would declare and speak of them. They are more than can be numbered.

40:11 Let Your lovingkindness and Your truth continually preserve me.

42:8 Lord You will command Your lovingkindness in the daytime and in the night Your song shall be with me.

43:2 For You are the God of my strength.

44:21 For You know the secrets of my heart.

45:6-7a Your throne, O God, is forever and ever; a scepter of righteousness is the scepter of Your Kingdom. You love righteousness and hate wickedness. . .

46:1-2 God, You are my refuge and strength, a very present help in trouble. Therefore I will not fear, even though the earth be removed, and though the mountains be carried into the midst of the sea.

46:10 You say: "Be still and know that I am God; I will be exalted among the nations, I will be exalted in the earth."

46:11 Lord of host You are with me; You are the God of Jacob and my refuge.

47:2-4 For You, Lord, Most High are awesome; You are a great King over all the earth. You will subdue the people under us, and the nations under our feet. You will choose my inheritance for me, the excellence of Jacob whom You love.

47:9b For the shields of the earth belong to You God; You are greatly exalted.

48:9-10 I have thought, O God, on Your lovingkindness in the midst of Your temple. According to Your name, O God, so is Your praise to the ends of the earth; Your right hand is full of righteousness.

48:14 For You are God, my God, forever and ever; You will be my guide even to death.

51:6 Behold, You desire truth in the inward parts and in the hidden part You will make me to know wisdom.

51:17 Your sacrifices God are a broken spirit, a broken and contrite heart. These O God, You will not despise.

53:2 God, You look down from heaven upon the children of men, to see if there are any who understand, who seek You.

54:4 Behold, God, You are my helper; Lord, You are who upholds my life.

55:18 And You shall hear my voice, You have redeemed my soul in peace from the battle that was against me.

55:22 I will cast my burden on You, Lord, and You shall sustain me; You shall never permit the righteous to be moved.

59:9-10 For God, You are my defense. You, God of mercy come to meet me.

59:16-17 For You have been my defense and refuge in the day of my trouble. To You, O my strength,

I will sing praise for You God. You are my defense. My God of mercy, I know you shall come to meet me.

61:3 For You have been a shelter for me, a strong tower from my enemies. I will trust in the shelter of Your wings.

62:2 You only are my rock and my salvation; You are my defense; I shall not be moved.

62:6 You only are my rock and my salvation; You are my defense; I shall not be moved.

62:7 You, God, are my salvation and my glory; You are the rock of my strength, and my refuge, is in You, God.

62:8 I will trust in You at all times, I will pour out my heart before You; God, You are a refuge for me.

62:12 Also to You, O Lord, belongs mercy; for You render to each one according to his work.

63:3 Because Your lovingkindness is better than life.

64:10 The righteous shall be glad in You, Lord, and trust You and all the upright in heart shall glorify You.

65:2 O You who hear my prayer.

65:4 Blessed is the man You choose and cause to approach You.

65:5 By awesome deeds in righteousness You will answer me, O God of my salvation. You are the confidence of all the ends of the earth, and of the far–off seas.

66:5 I come and see Your works God; You are awesome in Your doing toward the sons of men.

66:7 You rule by Your power forever, Your eyes observe the nations.

66:9 Who keeps my soul among the living and does not allow my feet to be moved?

68:5 A father of the fatherless, a defender of widows is You, God, in Your holy habitation.

68:10 You, O God, provided from Your goodness for the poor.

68:11 Lord, You gave the word; great is the company of those who proclaimed it.

68:13 You will be like the wings of a dove covered with silver and her feathers with yellow gold.

68:19 Blessed be to You, Lord, who daily loads me with benefits, You are the God of my salvation.

68:20 My God, You are the God of salvation; and to You, my Lord, belong escapes from death.

68:35 O God, You are more awesome than your holy places. You are the God of Israel who gives strength and power to Your people. Blessed be God!

69:16 Hear me, O Lord, for Your lovingkindness is good; turn to me according to the multitude of Your tender mercies.

69:32-33 The humble shall see this and be glad; and we who seek You God, our hearts shall live. For You, Lord, hear the poor and do not despise prisoners of this world.

70:4 Let all those who seek You rejoice and be glad in You; and let those who love Your salvation say continually, let God be magnified.

71:3-4 For You are my strong refuge, to which I may resort continually; You have given the commandment to save me, For You are my rock and my fortress.

71:5-7 For You are my hope, O Lord God; You are my trust from my youth. By You I have been upheld from birth; You are He who took me out of my mothers womb. My praise shall be continually of You. You have become as a wonder to many. You are my strong refuge.

71:17-18 O God, You have taught me from my youth; and to this day I declare Your wondrous works. Now also, when I am old and grayheaded, O God, do not forsake me, until I declare Your strength to this generation.

71:19 Your righteousness, O God, is very high, You who have done great things. Oh God, who is like You?

71:24 My tongue shall talk of Your righteousness all the day long.

72:17-19 Your name shall endure forever; Your name shall continue as long as the sun and men shall be blessed in You; all nations shall call You blessed. Blessed be the Lord God, the God of Israel, who only does wondrous things! And blessed be Your glorious name forever! And let the whole earth be filled with Your glory. Amen and Amen.

73:24 You hold me by my right hand. You will guide me with Your counsel and afterward receive me to glory.

73:25 Whom have I in heaven but You? And there is non upon earth that I desire besides You.

73:26 God, You are the strength of my heart and my portion forever.

73:28 It is good for me to draw near to You God; I have put my trust in You, Lord God, that I may declare all Your works.

74:12 For God, You are my King from of old, working salvation in the midst of the earth.

74:16 The day is Yours, the night also is Yours. You have prepared the light and the sun. You have set all the borders of the earth. You have made summer and winter.

76:4 You are more excellent and glorious than the mountains of prey.

76:7 You, Yourself, are to be feared; and who may stand in Your presence when once You are angry?

77:13-15 Who is so great a God as our God? You are the God who does wonders; You have declared Your strength among the people. You have with Your arm redeemed Your people.

78:7 That I may set my hope in You God, and not forget Your works.

78:35 Then I remembered that You, God, are my rock and the Most High God, my redeemer.

78:38 But You, being full of compassion, forgave my iniquity and did not destroy me.

78:53 You lead me on safely, so I will not fear.

81:13-14 Oh that I, Your child, would listen to You and walk in Your ways. You would soon subdue my enemies, and turn Your hand against my adversaries.

84:9-10 O God, behold You are my shield, and look upon the face of Your anointed. For a day in Your courts is better than a thousand. I would rather be a door keeper in Your house, my God, than dwell in the tents of wickedness.

84:11 For You, Lord God, are a sun and shield; Lord You will give grace and glory; no good thing will You withhold from those who walk uprightly.

85:8 I will hear what You, my Lord, will speak. For You will speak peace to Your people and to Your saints.

86:5 For You, Lord, are good and ready to forgive and abundant in mercy to all those who call upon You.

86:10 For You are great, and do wondrous things, You alone are God.

86:13 For great is Your mercy toward me, and You have delivered my soul from the depths of Sheol.

89:2a, 5 Your faithfulness You shall establish in the very heavens. And the heavens will praise Your wonders, O Lord.

89:7-8 God, You are greatly to be feared in the assembly of the saints, and to be held in reverence by all those around You. O Lord,

God of hosts, who is mighty like You, O Lord? Your faithfulness also surrounds You.

89:11 The heavens are Yours, the earth also is Yours; the world and all its fullness, You have founded them.

89:14 Righteousness and justice are the foundation of Your throne; mercy and truth go before Your face.

89:17-18 For You are the glory of my strength. For my shield belongs to the Lord.

90:1-2 Lord, You have been my dwelling place in all generations. Before the mountains were brought forth, or ever You had formed the earth and the world. Even from everlasting to everlasting, You are God.

91:4 You shall cover me with Your feathers, and under Your wing I shall take refuge, Your truth shall be my shield and buckler.

91:14-16 Because You have set Your love upon me, therefore You will deliver me; You will set me on high, because I have known Your name. I shall call upon You, and You will answer me; You will be with me in trouble; You will deliver me and honor me. With long life You will satisfy me, and show me Your salvation.

92:5 O Lord, how great are Your works! Your thoughts are very deep.

92:15 You are my rock, and there is no unrighteousness in You.

93:2, 5 Your throne is established from of old; You are from everlasting. Your testimonies are very sure; Holiness adorns Your house, O Lord, forever.

94:11-12 Lord, You know my thoughts, that they are futile. I am blessed because You instruct me, O Lord.

94:14-15 For You, Lord, will not cast me off, nor will You forsake me because I am Your inheritance. But judgment will return to righteousness and all the upright in heart will follow it.

94:22 But You, Lord, have been my defense, and my God, the rock of my refuge.

95:3 For You, Lord, are the great God, and great King above all gods.

96:4 For You, Lord, are great and greatly to be praised; You are to be feared above all gods.

97:2-6 Clouds and darkness surround You; righteousness and justice are the foundation of Your throne. A fire goes before You; and burns up Your enemies round about. Your lightnings light the world; the earth sees and trembles. The mountains melt like wax at Your presence, Lord. The heavens declare Your righteousness, and all the people see Your glory.

97:10-12 We who love You, Lord, hate evil! You preserve the souls of Your saints; You deliver me out of the hand of the wicked. Light is sown for the righteous, and gladness for the upright in heart. I will rejoice in You, Lord, and give thanks at the remembrance of Your holy name.

98:2-3 You, Lord, have made known Your salvation; Your righteousness You have revealed in the sight of the nations. You have remembered Your mercy and Your faithfulness to the house of Israel.

98:9 For You are coming to judge the earth. With righteousness You shall judge the world.

99:8 You answered me O Lord my God; You are to me the God who forgives.

100:3 I know that You, Lord, You are God; it is You who has made me and not myself. We are Your children and the sheep of Your pasture.

100:5 For You, Lord, are good; Your mercy is everlasting, and Your truth endures to all generations.

102:12 But You O Lord, Shall endure forever, and the remembrance of Your name to all generations.

102:27 But You are the same, and Your years will have no end.

103:2-5 Bless the Lord, O my soul, and forget not all Your benefits; who forgives all my iniquities, who heals all my diseases. Who redeems my life from destruction, who crowns me with lovingkindness and tender mercies, who satisfies my mouth with good things, so that my youth is renewed like the eagle's.

103:6 Lord, You execute righteousness and justice for all who are oppressed.

103:8 Lord, You are merciful and gracious, slow to anger, and abounding in mercy.

103:11-12 For as the heavens are high above the earth, so great is Your mercy toward those who fear You. As far as the east is from the west, so far have You removed my transgressions from me.

103:13-14 As a father shows compassion for his children, so You, Lord, are compassionate toward me. I fear and respect You, because You know my frame; You remember that I am dust.

103:17 Your mercy Lord is from

every lasting to everlasting on me because I choose to fear and respect You.

104:1 Bless You, Lord, O my soul! O Lord, my God, You are very great; You are clothed with honor and majesty.

104:24 O Lord, how diverse are Your works! In wisdom you have made them all. The earth is full of Your possessions.

104:28-30 You open Your hand and I am filled with good. You hide Your face, and I am troubled; You take away my breath, and I die and return to dust. You send forth Your Spirit, and I was created.

105:3-5 Let my heart rejoice and seek You, Lord; I seek You, Lord, and Your strength; I shall seek Your face evermore! I will remember Your marvelous works which You have done.

105:8 You remember Your covenant forever, the word which You commanded, for a thousand generations.

106:1 Oh I shall give thanks to You, Lord, for You are good! For Your mercy endures forever.

106:4 Remember me O Lord, with the favor You have toward your people. Oh visit me with Your salvation, that I may see the benefit of Your chosen ones, that I may rejoice in the gladness of Your nation, that I may glory with Your inheritance.

106:44-45 You regarded my afflictions, when You heard my cry; and for my sake You remembered Your covenant, and relented according to the multitude of Your mercies.

106:48 Blessed be You, Lord, God of Israel—from everlasting to everlasting!

107:1 I give thanks to You, Lord, for You are good! For Your mercy endures forever.

107:41-43 You set the poor on high, far from affliction, and make our families like a flock. The righteous see it and rejoice, and all iniquity stops its mouth. Whoever is wise will observe these things, and we will understand the lovingkindness of You, Lord.

108:4 For Your mercy is great above the heavens, and Your truth reaches to the clouds.

111:3-5 Your work is honorable and glorious, and Your righteousness endures forever. Lord, You are gracious and full of compassion. You will ever be mindful of Your covenant.

111:7-8 The works of Your hands are verity and justice. All Your precepts are sure, they stand fast

forever and ever.

111:10 The fear of You, Lord, is the beginning of wisdom.

113:5-8 Who is like You, Lord, my God, who dwells on high, who humbles Himself to behold the things that are in the heavens and in the earth? You raise the poor out of the dust, and lift the needy out of the ash heap. That You may seat me with princes—with the princes of Your people.

115:11 I am one who fears You, Lord, I trust in You: You are my help and my shield.

116:5 Gracious are You, Lord, and righteous, yes, You God, are merciful.

118:1 Oh I give thanks to You, Lord, for You are good! For Your mercy endures forever.

118:8 It is better to trust in You, Lord, than to put confidence in men.

119:64 The earth, O Lord is full of Your mercy; teach me Your statutes.

119:73 Your hands have made me and fashioned me; give me understanding that I may learn Your commandments.

119:89-90 Forever, O Lord, Your word is settled in heaven. Your faithfulness endures to all generations; You established the earth, and it abides.

119:103 How sweet are Your words to my taste, sweeter than honey to my mouth.

119:105 Your word is a lamp to my feet and a light to my path.

119:130 The entrance of Your words gives light, it gives understanding to the simple.

119:132 Look upon me and be merciful to me, as Your custom is toward those who love Your name.

119:137-138 Righteous are You O Lord, and upright are Your judgments. Your testimonies, which You have commanded, are righteous and very faithful.

119:140-144 Your word is very pure; therefore as Your servant I love it. I am small and despised, yet I do not forget Your precepts. Your righteousness is an everlasting righteousness, and Your law is truth. Trouble and anguish have overtaken me, yet Your commandments are my delights. The righteousness of Your testimonies is everlasting; give me understanding, and I shall live.

119:151-152 You are near O Lord, and all Your commandments are truth. Concerning Your testimonies I have known of old that You have founded them forever.

119:156 Great are Your tender mercies, O Lord; revive me according to Your judgments.

119:160 The entirety of Your word is truth, and every one of Your righteous judgments endures forever.

121:4 Behold You who keeps Israel shall neither slumber nor sleep.

130:3-4 If You, Lord, should mark iniquities, O Lord who could stand? But there is forgiveness with You, that You may be feared.

135:6 Whatever You please Lord, You do, in heaven and in earth.

134:13-14 Your name, O Lord, endures forever, Your fame, O Lord, throughout all generations. For You, Lord, will judge Your people and You will have compassion on Your servants.

144:1-2 Blessed be the Lord my rock. My lovingkindness and my fortress, my high tower and my deliverer, my shield and the one in whom I take refuge.

144:3-4 Lord, what am I, that You take knowledge of me? Or the son of man, that You are mindful of him? I am like a breath; my days are like a passing shadow.

145:5 I will meditate on the

glorious splendor of Your majesty, and on Your wondrous works.

145:8 Lord, You are gracious and full of compassion, slow to anger and great in mercy. Lord, You are good to all, and Your tender mercies are over all Your works.

145:13 Your Kingdom is an everlasting kingdom, and Your dominion endures throughout all generations.

145:17-20 Lord You are righteous in all Your ways, gracious in all Your works. Lord You are near to all who call upon You, to all who call upon You in truth. You will fulfill the desire of those who fear You; You also will hear my cry and save me. Lord, You preserve all those who love You, but all the wicked You will destroy.

146:8-10 Lord, You open the eyes of the blind, You raise those who are bowed down, You love the righteous, You watch over the stranger, You relieve the fatherless and widow, but the way of the wicked You turn upside down. You, Lord, shall reign forever — You are my God, O Zion, and to all generations.

147:3-6 You heal my broken heart, and bind up my wounds. You count the number of the stars; You call them all by name. Great are You, Lord, and mighty in power; Your

understanding is infinite. You, Lord, lift up the humble; You cast the wicked down to the ground.

147:11 You, Lord, take pleasure in those who fear You, in those of us who hope in Your mercy.

147:13-18 For You have strengthened the bars of your gates, You have blessed Your children. You makes peace in Your borders, and fill us with the finest wheat. You send out Your command to the earth; Your word runs very swiftly. You give snow like wool, You scatter the frost like ashes; You cast out hail like morsels; who can stand before Your cold? You send out Your word and melt them; You cause Your wind to blow, and the waters to flow.

148:5-6 Let me praise Your name Lord, for You commanded and it was created. You also established Your creation forever and ever; You made a decree which shall not pass away.

149:4-5 For You, Lord, take pleasure in me Your child; You will beautify the humble with salvation. As Your saint I shall be joyful in glory; I shall sing aloud on my bed. I shall give high praises of You God, with my mouth.

Chapter 3

CONFESSION

5:1-3 Give ear to my words, O Lord, consider my meditation. Give heed to the voice of my cry, my King and my God, for to You I will pray. My voice You shall hear in the morning, O Lord; In the morning I will direct it to You, and I will look up.

5:7 But as for me, I will come into Your house in the multitude of Your mercy; In fear of You I will worship toward Your holy temple.

7:9-10 For the righteous You test our hearts and minds; my defense is of You God, who saves the upright in heart.

11:4 Lord You are in Your holy temple, Your throne is in heaven; Your eyes behold, Your eyelids test the sons of men.

14:2 Lord You look down from heaven upon the children of men, to see if there are any of us who understand, who seek God.

16:1-2 Preserve me, O God, for in You I put my trust. O my soul, I have said to You, Lord, "You are my Lord, my goodness is nothing apart from You."

16:8-9 I have set the Lord always before me; because You are at my right hand I shall not be moved. Therefore my heart is glad, and my glory rejoices; my flesh also will rest in hope.

17:2 Let my vindication come from Your presence; let Your eyes look on the things that are upright.

17:3 You have tested my heart; You have visited me in the night; You have tried me and have found nothing; I have purposed that my mouth shall not transgress.

18:1-3 I will love You, O Lord, my strength. Lord, You are my rock and my fortress and my deliverer; my God, my strength, in whom I will trust; my shield and the horn of my salvation, my stronghold. I will call upon You, Lord, who is worthy to be praised; so shall I be saved from my enemies.

18:20 Lord, You reward me according to my righteousness;

according to the cleanness of my hand.

18:25-27 With the merciful You will show Yourself merciful; with a blameless man You will show Yourself blameless; with the pure You will show Yourself pure; and with the devious You will show Yourself shrewd. For You will save the humble people, but will bring down haughty looks.

19:12 Who can understand his errors? Cleanse me from secret faults. Keep back Your servant also from presumptuous sins; let them not have dominion over me. Then I shall be blameless, and I shall be innocent of great transgression.

19:14 Let the words of my mouth and the meditation of my heart be acceptable in Your sight, O Lord, my strength and my Redeemer.

24:3-5 Who may ascend into the hill of the Lord? Or who may stand in Your holy place? He who has clean hands and a pure heart, who has not lifted up his soul to an idol, nor sworn deceitfully. He shall receive blessing from the Lord, and righteousness from the God of his salvation.

25:4-7 Show me Your ways, O Lord; teach me Your paths. Lead me in Your truth and teach me, for You are the God of my salvation; on You I wait all the day.

Remember, O Lord, Your tender mercies and Your lovingkindness, for they are from of old. Do not remember the sins of my youth, nor my transgressions; according to Your mercy remember me, for Your goodness' sake, O Lord.

25:8-9 Good and upright is the Lord; therefore You teach sinners in the way. The humble You guide in justice, and the humble You teach Your way.

25:10-11 All the paths of the Lord are mercy and truth, to such as keep Your covenant and Your testimonies. For Your name's sake, O Lord, pardon my iniquity, for it is great.

25:14 The secret of the Lord is with those who fear Him, and You will show them Your covenant.

25:16-18 Turn Yourself to me, and have mercy on me, for I am desolate and afflicted. The troubles of my heart have enlarged; bring me out of my distresses! Look on my affliction and my pain, and forgive all my sins.

26:2-3 Examine me, O Lord, and prove me; try my mind and my heart. For Your lovingkindness is before my eyes, and I have walked in Your truth.

26:9, 11-12 Do not gather my soul with sinners, nor my life with bloodthirsty men, but as for me, I will walk in my integrity; redeem me and be merciful to me. My foot stands in an even place; in the congregations I will bless the Lord.

27:1 Lord, You are my light and my salvation; whom shall I fear? Lord, You are the strength of my life; of whom shall I be afraid?

27:11 Teach me Your way, O Lord, and lead me in a smooth path, because of my enemies.

30:5 For Your anger is but for a moment, Your favor is for life; weeping may endure for a night, but joy comes in the morning.

30:6-7 Now in my prosperity I said, "I shall never be moved." Lord, by Your favor You have made my mountain stand strong; You hid Your face, and I was troubled.

31:3 For You are my rock and my fortress; therefore, for Your name's sake, lead me and guide me.

31:5 Into Your hand I commit my spirit; You have redeemed me, O Lord, God of truth.

31:14-17 But as for me, I trust in You, O Lord; I say, "You are my God." My times are in Your hand; deliver me from the hand of my enemies, and from those who persecute me. Make Your face

shine upon Your servant; save me for Your mercies' sake. Do not let me be ashamed, O Lord, for I have called upon You; let the wicked be ashamed; let them be silent in the grave.

32:4-5 For day and night Your hand was heavy upon me; my vitality was turned into the drought of summer. I acknowledged my sin to You, and my iniquity I have not hidden. I said, "I will confess my transgressions to You, Lord," and You will forgive the iniquity of my sin.

33:13-15 The Lord looks from heaven; You see all the sons of men. From the place of Your dwelling You look on all the inhabitants of the earth; You fashion their hearts individually; You consider all their works.

37:37 Mark the blameless man, and observe the upright; for the future of that man is peace.

38:9-10 Lord, all my desire is before You; and my sighing is not hidden from You. My heart pants, my strength fails me; as for the light of my eyes, it also has gone from me.

39:7 And now, Lord, what do I wait for? My hope is in You.

39:8 Deliver me from all my transgressions; do not make me

the reproach of the foolish.

39:12 Hear my prayer, O Lord, and give ear to my cry; do not be silent at my tears; for I am a stranger with You, a sojourner, as all my fathers were.

40:8-12 I delight to do Your will, O my God, and Your law is within my heart. I have proclaimed the good news of righteousness in the great assembly; indeed, I do not restrain my lips, O Lord, You Yourself know. I have not hidden Your righteousness within my heart; I have declared Your faithfulness and Your salvation; I have not concealed Your lovingkindness and Your truth from the great assembly. Do not withhold Your tender mercies from me, O Lord; let Your lovingkindness and Your truth continually preserve me. For innumerable evils have surrounded me; my iniquities have overtaken me, so that I am not able to look up; they are more than the hairs of my head; therefore my heart fails me.

41:4 I said, "Lord, be merciful to me; heal my soul, for I have sinned against You."

41:11-12 By this I know that You are well pleased with me, because my enemy does not triumph over me. As for me, You uphold me in my integrity, and set me before Your face forever.

42:1-2 As the deer pants for the water brooks, so pants my soul for You, O God. My soul thirsts for God, for the living God. When shall I come and appear before God?

44:6-7 For I will not trust in my bow, nor shall my sword save me. But You have saved me from my enemies, and have put to shame those who hated me.

44:21 You know the secrets of the heart.

51:1-2 Have mercy upon me, O God, according to Your lovingkindness; according to the multitude of Your tender mercies, blot out my transgressions. Wash me thoroughly from my iniquity, and cleanse me from my sin.

51:3-4 For I acknowledge my transgressions, and my sin is always before me. Against You, You only, have I sinned, and done this evil in Your sight — That You may be found just when You speak, and blameless when You judge.

51:6-9 Behold, You desire truth in the inward parts, and in the hidden part You will make me to know wisdom. Purge me with hyssop, and I shall be clean; wash me, and I shall be whiter than snow. Make me hear joy and gladness that the bones You have broken may rejoice. Hide Your face from my sins, and blot out all my iniquities.

51:10-12 Create in me a clean heart, O God, and renew a steadfast spirit within me. Do not cast me away from Your presence, and do not take Your Holy Spirit from me. Restore to me the joy of Your salvation, and uphold me by Your generous Spirit. Then I will teach transgressors Your ways, and sinners shall be converted to You.

51:14-17 Deliver me from the guilt of bloodshed, O God, the God of my salvation, and my tongue shall sing aloud of Your righteousness. O Lord, open my lips, and my mouth shall show forth Your praise. For You do not desire sacrifice, or else I would give it; You do not delight in burnt offering. The sacrifice You desire God, is a broken spirit, a broken and a contrite heart — these, O God, You will not despise.

55:16-17 As for me, I will call upon God, and You, Lord, shall save me. Evening and morning and at noon I will pray, and cry aloud, and You shall hear my voice.

62:1 Truly my soul silently waits for You God; from You comes my salvation. You only are my rock and my salvation; You are my defense; I shall not be greatly moved.

66:10 For You, O God, have tested me; You have refined me as silver is refined.

66:16-20 I will declare what You have done for my soul. I cried to You with my mouth, and I extoll with my tongue. If I regard iniquity in my heart, You, Lord, will not hear. But certainly God, You have heard me; You have attended to the voice of my prayer. Blessed be to You God, who has not turned away my prayer, nor Your mercy from me!

69:5 O God, You know my foolishness; and my sins are not hidden from You.

69:13 But as for me, my prayer is to You, O Lord, in the acceptable time; O God, in the multitude of Your mercy, hear me in the truth of Your salvation.

80:3 Restore me, O God; cause Your face to shine, and I shall be saved!

84:2 My soul longs, yes, even faints for Your courts Lord; my heart and my flesh cry out for You the living God.

85:8-9 I will hear what You God, my Lord, will speak. For You will speak peace to Your people and to Your saints; but let me not turn back to folly. Surely Your salvation is near to those who fear You that glory may dwell in my life.

89:30-34 If I forsake Your law and do not walk in Your judgments, If I break Your statutes and do not keep Your commandments, Then You will punish my transgression with the rod, and my iniquity with stripes. Nevertheless Your lovingkindness will not be utterly take from me, nor will You allow Your faithfulness to fail. Your covenant You will not break, nor alter the word that has gone out of Your lips.

94:9-15 You, who planted the ear, shall You not hear? You, who formed the eye, shall You not see? You, who instructs the nations, shall You, not correct, You who teaches man knowledge? Lord, You know the thoughts of man, that they are futile. Blessed is the man whom You instruct, O Lord, and teach out of Your law, That You may give me rest from the days of adversity, until the pit is dug for the wicked. For You, Lord, will not cast off Your people, nor will You forsake Your inheritance. But judgment will return to righteousness, and all the upright in heart will follow it.

118:18 Lord, You have chastened me severely, but You have not given me over to death.

119:10-11 With my whole heart I have sought You; oh, let me not wander from Your commandments! Your word I have hidden in my heart that I might not sin against You.

119:15-16 I will meditate on Your precepts, and contemplate Your ways. I will delight myself in Your statutes; I will not forget Your word.

119:30-31 I have chosen the way of truth; Your judgments I have laid before me. I cling to Your testimonies; O Lord, do not put me to shame!

119:37 Turn away my eyes from looking at worthless things.

119:39-43 Turn away my reproach, which I dread, for Your judgments are good. Behold, I long for Your precepts; revive me in Your righteousness. So shall I have an answer for him who reproaches me, for I trust in Your word. And take not the word of truth utterly out of my mouth, for I have hope in Your ordinances.

119:45 I will walk at liberty, for I seek Your precepts.

119:47-50 I will delight myself in Your commandments, which I love. My hands also I will lift up to Your commandments, which I love, and I will meditate on Your statutes. Remember the word to Your servant, upon which You have caused me to hope. This is my comfort in my affliction, for Your word has given me life.

119:57-58 You are my portion, O Lord; I have said that I would keep Your words. I entreated Your favor with my whole heart; be merciful to me according to Your word.

119:64 The earth, O Lord, is full of Your mercy; teach me Your statutes.

119:67 Before I was afflicted I went astray, but now I keep Your word.

119:71 It is good for me that I have been afflicted, that I may learn Your statutes.

119:80 Let my heart be blameless regarding Your statutes, that I may not be ashamed.

119:92-94 Unless Your law had been my delight, I would then have perished in my affliction. I will never forget Your precepts, for by them You have given me life. I am Yours, save me; for I have sought Your precepts. That I may keep Your word.

119:102-103 I have not departed from Your judgments, for You Yourself have taught me. How sweet are Your words to my taste, sweeter than honey to my mouth!

119:110 The wicked have laid a snare for me, yet I have not strayed from Your precepts.

121:7-8 Lord, You shall preserve me from all evil; You shall preserve my soul. Lord, You shall preserve my going out and my coming in from this time forth, and even forevermore.

125:2 As the mountains surround Jerusalem, so You, Lord, surround Your people from this time forth and forever

127:1 Unless You, Lord, build the house, I labor in vain building it; unless You, Lord, guard the city, the watchman stays awake in vain.

130:4-5 But there is forgiveness with You, that You may be feared. I wait for You, Lord, my soul waits, and in Your word I do hope.

139:1-2 O Lord, You have searched me and known me. You know my sitting down and my rising up; You understand my thought afar off.

139:7 Where can I go from Your Spirit? Or where can I flee from Your presence?

139:23-24 Search me, O God, and know my heart; try me, and know my anxieties; and see if there is any wicked way in me, and lead me in the way everlasting.

Chapter 4

COMFORT

for the oppressed, a refuge in times of trouble. And I, who know Your name will put my trust in You; for You, Lord, will not forsake those who seek You.

9:12 When You avenge blood, You remember me; You do not forget the cry of the humble.

10:1 Why do You stand afar off, O Lord? Why do You hide in times of trouble?

3:4 I cried to You, Lord, with my voice, and You heard me from Your holy hill. I lay down and slept; I awoke, for You, Lord, sustained me. I will not be afraid of ten thousand people who have set themselves against me all around.

3:7 Arise, O Lord; save me, O my God!

4:3 But I know that You, Lord, have set apart for Yourself those who are godly; You, Lord, will hear when I call to You.

4:6-7 Who will show me any good? Lord lift up the light of Your countenance upon me. You have put gladness in my heart.

4:8 I will both lie down in peace and sleep for You alone, O Lord, make me dwell in safety.

5:7 But as for me, I will come into Your house in the multitude of Your mercy; in fear of You I will worship toward Your holy temple.

9:9-10 You, Lord, will be a refuge

10:12 Arise, O Lord! O God, lift up Your hand! Do not forget me for I am humble.

10:14 But You have seen, for You observe trouble and grief, to repay it by Your hand. I am helpless, I commit myself to You; for You are the helper of the fatherless.

10:17-18 Lord, You have heard the desire of the humble; You will prepare my heart; You will cause Your ear to hear, to do justice to the fatherless and the oppressed, that the man of the earth may oppress me no more.

11:4 You, Lord, are in Your holy temple, Your throne is in heaven; Your eyes behold, Your eyelids test the sons of men.

14:2 Lord You look down from heaven upon the children of men, to see if there are any who understand, who seek You.

16:5 O Lord, You are the portion of my inheritance and my cup; You maintain my lot.

16:11 You will show me the path of life; in Your presence is fullness of joy; at Your right hand are pleasures forevermore.

17:5 Uphold my steps in Your paths, that my footsteps may not slip.

17:8-9 Keep me as the apple of Your eye; Hide me under the shadow of Your wings, from the wicked who oppress me, from my deadly enemies who surround me.

17:15 As for me, I will see Your face in righteousness; I shall be satisfied when I awake in Your likeness.

18:1-3 I will love You, O Lord, my strength. You, Lord, are my rock and my fortress and my deliverer; my God, my strength, in whom I will trust; my shield and the horn of my salvation, my stronghold. I will call upon You, Lord, who is worthy to be praised; so shall I be saved from my enemies.

18:6 In my distress I called upon You, Lord, and cried out to You, my God; You heard my voice from Your temple, and my cry came before You, even to Your ears.

18:18-20 They confronted me in the day of my calamity, but You, Lord, are my support. You also brought me out into a broad place; You delivered me because You delighted in me.

18:36 You enlarged my path under me, so my feet do not slip.

18:39 For You have armed me with strength for the battle; You have subdued under me those who rose up against me.

18:48 You deliver me from my enemies. You also lift me up above those who rise against me; You have delivered me from the violent man.

20:1-6 May You, Lord, answer me in the day of trouble; may Your name, God of Jacob defend me; may You send your help from the sanctuary, and strengthen me out of Zion; may You remember all my offerings, and accept my burnt sacrifice. May You grant to me according to Your heart's desire, and fulfill my purpose. I will rejoice in Your salvation, and in Your name I will set up a banner! May You, Lord, fulfill all my petitions. Now I know that You, Lord, save Your anointed; You will answer me from Your holy heaven with the saving strength of Your right hand.

23rd Psalm - Lord, You are my shepherd; I shall not want. You make me to lie down in green pastures; You lead me beside the still waters. You restore my soul; You lead me in the paths of righteousness for Your name's sake. Yea, though I walk through the valley of the shadow of death, I will fear no evil; for You are with me; Your rod and Your staff, they comfort me. You prepare a table before me in the presence of my enemies; You anoint my head with oil; my cup runs over. Surely goodness and mercy shall follow me all the days of my life; and I will dwell in Your house Lord, forever.

25:1 To You, O Lord, I lift up my soul. O my God, I trust in You.

27:14 I will wait on You, Lord; I will be of good courage, and You shall strengthen my heart; I shall wait, I say, on You, Lord!

27:4-6 One thing I have desired of You, Lord, that will I seek: That I may dwell in Your house, all the days of my life, to behold the beauty of You, Lord, and to inquire in Your temple. For in the time of trouble You shall hide me in Your pavilion; in the secret place of Your tabernacle You shall hide me; You shall set me high upon a rock.

28:8 Lord, You are my strength, and You are the saving refuge of Your anointed.

30:1-3 I will extol You, O Lord, for You have lifted me up, and have not let my foes rejoice over me. O Lord my God, I cried out to You, and You healed me. O Lord, You brought my soul up from the grave; You have kept me alive, that I should not go down to the pit.

30:10-12 Hear, O Lord, and have mercy on me; Lord, be my helper! You have turned for me my mourning into dancing; You have put off my sackcloth and clothed me with gladness, to the end that my glory may sing praise to You and not be silent. O Lord my God, I will give thanks to You forever.

31:7-8 I will be glad and rejoice in Your mercy, for You have considered my trouble; You have known my soul in adversities, and have not shut me up into the hand of the enemy; You have set my feet in a wide place.

31:19 Oh, how great is Your goodness, which You have laid up for those who fear You. Which You have prepared for those who trust in You. In the presence of the sons of men!

31:23-24 Oh, I love You, Lord, I with all of Your saints! For You, Lord, preserve the faithful, and fully repay the proud person. I will be of good courage, and You shall strengthen my heart, I and all who hope in You, Lord.

32:7 You are my hiding place; You shall preserve me from trouble; You shall surround me with songs of deliverance.

32:10-11 Many sorrows shall be to the wicked; but I trust in You, Lord. Your mercy shall surround me. I will be glad in You, Lord, and rejoice and shout for joy. With all those who are upright in heart!

34:9-10 There is no want to those who fear You. The young lions lack and suffer hunger; but those who seek You, Lord, shall not lack any good thing.

34:18 Lord, You are near to those who have a broken heart, and save such as have a contrite spirit.

34:19-20, 22 Many are the afflictions of the righteous, but You, Lord, deliver me out of them all. You guard all my bones; not one of them is broken. Lord, You redeem the soul of Your servants, and none of those who trust in You shall be condemned.

35:9 And my soul shall be joyful in You, Lord. It shall rejoice in Your salvation. All my bones shall say, Lord, who is like you.

37:3-4 I shall trust in You, Lord, and do good; I will dwell in the land, and feed on Your faithfulness. I delight myself also in You, Lord, and You shall give me the desires of my heart.

37:5 If I commit my ways to You, Lord, trust also in You, You shall bring my desires to pass. You shall bring forth righteousness as the light, and Your justice as the noonday.

37:7, 8 I shall rest in You, Lord, and wait patiently for You; I shall cease from anger, and forsake wrath; I will not fret—as it only causes harm.

37:11 But the meek shall inherit the earth, and shall delight ourselves in the abundance of peace.

37:23-24 The steps of a good man are ordered by You, Lord, and You delight in my ways. Though I fall, I shall not be utterly cast down; for You, Lord, will uphold me with Your hand.

37:28-29 For You, Lord, loves justice, and do not forsake Your saints; I am preserved forever. But the descendants of the wicked shall be cut off. The righteous shall inherit the land, and dwell in it forever.

37:34 I shall wait on You, Lord, and keep Your way, and You shall exalt me to inherit the land; when the wicked are cut off, I shall see it.

40:1-3 I waited patiently for You, Lord; and You inclined to me, and heard my cry. You also brought me up out of a horrible pit, out of the miry clay, and set my feet upon a rock, and established my steps. You have put a new song in my mouth — Praise to You, my God. Many will see You and fear, and will trust in You, Lord.

46:1-3 God, You are my refuge and strength, a very present help in trouble. Therefore I will not fear, even though the earth be removed, and though the mountains be carried into the midst of the sea; though its waters roar and be troubled, though the mountains shake with its swelling.

46:7 You, Lord of hosts, are with me; You the God of Jacob, are my refuge.

46:10 Be still, and know that I am God; I will be exalted among the nations, I will be exalted in the earth!

49:15 But God, You will redeem my soul from the power of the grave, for You shall receive me.

50:15 I call upon You in the day of trouble; You will deliver me, and I shall glorify You.

50:23 Whoever offers praise glorifies You; and to him who orders his conduct aright You will show Your salvation, God."

56:3-4 Whenever I am afraid, I will trust in You. In You God, I will praise Your word, In You God ,I have put my trust; I will not fear. What can flesh do to me?

56:8-11 You number my wanderings; put my tears into Your bottle; are they not in Your book? When I cry out to You, my enemies will turn back; this I know, because God, You are for me. In You God, I will praise Your word, In You, Lord I will praise Your word, In You God, I have put my trust; I will not be afraid. What can man do to me?

56:13 For You have delivered my soul from death. Have You not kept my feet from falling, that I may walk before You God, in the light of the living?

59:9 I will wait for You, O You my strength; for You God, are my defense.

59:16-17 But I will sing of Your power; yes, I will sing aloud of Your mercy in the morning; for You have been my defense and refuge in the day of my trouble. To You, O my Strength, I will sing praises; for You God, are my defense, my God of mercy.

61:4 I will abide in Your tabernacle forever; I will trust in the shelter of Your wings.

62:5-7 My soul waits silently for You alone, for my expectation is from You. You only are my rock and my salvation; You are my defense; I shall not be moved. In You, God, is my salvation and my glory; You are the rock of my strength, and my refuge, is in You.

63:1-5 O God, You are my God; will I seek You; my soul thirsts for You; my flesh longs for You in a dry and thirsty land where there is no water. So I have looked for You in the sanctuary, I see Your power and Your glory. Because Your lovingkindness is better than life, My lips shall praise You. Thus I will bless You while I live; I will lift up my hands in Your name. My soul shall be satisfied as with marrow and fatness, and my mouth shall praise You with joyful lips.

65:5-7 By Your awesome deeds in righteousness You will answer me, God of my salvation, You who are the confidence of all the ends of the earth, and of the far-off seas; who established the mountains by Your strength, being clothed with power; You who still the noise of the seas, the noise of their waves, and the tumult of the people.

71:18-21 Now also when I am old and gray headed, O God, do not forsake me, until I declare Your strength to this generation, Your power to everyone who is to come. Also Your righteousness, O God, is very high, You who have done great things; O God, who is like You? You, who have shown me great and severe troubles, shall revive me again, and bring me up again from the depths of the earth. You shall increase my greatness, and comfort me on every side.

73:24-26 You will guide me with Your counsel, and afterward receive me to glory. Whom have I in heaven but You? And there is none upon earth that I desire besides You. My flesh and my heart fail; but God, You are the strength of my heart and my portion forever.

73:28 But it is good for me to draw near to You God; I have put my trust in You, Lord, God, that I may declare all Your works.

84:5 Blessed is the man whose strength is in You, whose heart is set on pilgrimage.

84:9-10 O God, You are my shield, and look upon the face of Your anointed. For a day in Your courts is better than a thousand.

I would rather be a doorkeeper in the house of my God than dwell in the tents of wickedness.

84:10-13 Mercy and truth have met together; righteousness and peace have kissed. Truth shall spring out of the earth; righteousness shall look down from heaven. Yes, Lord You will give what is good; and our land will yield its increase. Righteousness will go before You, and shall make Your footsteps my pathway.

86:11-13 Teach me Your way, O Lord; I will walk in Your truth; unite my heart to fear Your name. I will praise You, O Lord my God, with all my heart, and I will glorify Your name forevermore. For great is Your mercy toward me, and You have delivered my soul from the depths of Sheol.

90:12-15 So teach me to number my days, that I may gain a heart of wisdom. Return, O Lord! How long? And have compassion on me Your servant. Oh, satisfy me early with Your mercy, that I may rejoice and be glad all of my days! Make me glad according to the days in which You have afflicted me, The years in which I have seen evil.

91:3-4 Surely You shall deliver me from the snare of the fowler and from the perilous pestilence. You shall cover me with Your feathers, and under Your wings I shall take refuge; Your truth shall be my shield and buckler.

91:7-9 A thousand may fall at my side, and ten thousand at my right hand; but it shall not come near me. Only with my eyes shall I look, and see the reward of the wicked. Because I have made You, Lord, who is my refuge, even the Most High, my dwelling place.

91:10-15 No evil shall befall me, nor shall any plague come near me for You shall give Your angels charge over me, to keep me in all my ways. In their hands they shall bear me up, dwelling; lest I dash my foot against a stone. I shall tread upon the lion and the cobra, the young lion and the serpent I shall trample underfoot. Because I have set my love upon You, therefore You will deliver me; You will set me on high, because I have known Your name. I shall call upon You, and You will answer me; You will be with me in trouble; You will deliver me and I will honor You.

94:17-19, 22 Unless You, Lord, have been my help, my soul would soon have settled in silence. If I say, "My foot slips," Your mercy, O Lord, will hold me up. In the multitude of my anxieties within me, Your comforts delight my soul. But You, Lord, have been my defense, and my God, the rock of my refuge.

97:10-12 Those who love You, Lord, hate evil! You preserve the souls of Your saints; You deliver me out of the hand of the wicked. Light is sown for the righteous, and gladness for the upright in heart. I will rejoice in You, Lord, you are righteous, and I give thanks at the remembrance of Your holy name.

105:3-5, 8 I glory in Your holy name; let the hearts of those rejoice who seek You, Lord! I seek You, Lord, and Your strength; I seek Your face evermore! I remember Your marvelous works, which You have done. All Your wonders, and the judgments of Your mouth. You remember Your covenant forever, the word which You commanded, for a thousand generations.

106:44-45 Nevertheless You regarded my affliction, when You heard my cry; and for my sake You remembered Your covenant, and relented according to the multitude of Your mercies.

116:1-7 I love You, Lord, because You have heard My voice and my supplications. Because You have inclined Your ear to me, I will call upon You as long as I live. The pains of death surrounded me, and the pangs of Sheol laid hold of me; I found trouble and sorrow. Then I called upon Your name Lord: "O Lord, I implore You, deliver my soul!" Gracious are You, Lord, and righteous; yes, my God, You are merciful. Lord, You preserve the simple; I was brought low, and You saved me. Return to your rest, O my soul, for You, Lord, have dealt bountifully with me.

118:8-9 It is better to trust in the Lord than to put confidence in man. It is better to trust in the Lord than to put confidence in princes.

118:14 Lord, You are my strength and song, and You have become my salvation.

119:75-76 I know, O Lord, that Your judgments are right, and that in faithfulness You have afflicted me. Let, I pray, Your merciful kindness be for my comfort, according to Your word to Your servant.

119:105 Your word is a lamp to my feet and a light to my path.

123:1-2 Unto You I lift up my eyes, O You who dwell in the heavens. Behold, my eyes, as your servant looks to Your hand my Master, as the eyes of a maid to the hand of her mistress. So my eyes look to You, Lord, my God, until You have mercy on me.

138:6-8 Though You, Lord, are on high, yet You regard the lowly; but the proud You know from afar. Though I walk in the midst of trouble, You will revive me; You will stretch out Your hand against the wrath of my enemies, and Your right hand will save me. Lord, You will perfect that which concerns me; Your mercy, O Lord, endures forever; do not forsake the works of Your hands.

139:13-18 For You formed my inward parts; You covered me in my mother's womb. I will praise You, for I am fearfully and wonderfully made; marvelous are Your works, and that my soul knows very well. My frame was not hidden from You, when I was made in secret, and skillfully wrought in the lowest parts of the earth. Your eyes saw my substance, being yet unformed. And in Your book they all were written, The days fashioned for me, when as yet there were none of them. How precious also are Your thoughts to me, O God! How great is the sum of them! If I should count them, they would be more in number than the sand; when I awake, I am still with You.

140:13 Surely the righteous shall give thanks to Your name; the upright shall dwell in Your presence.

145:8-9 Lord, You are gracious and full of compassion, slow to anger and great in mercy. Lord, You are good to all, and Your tender mercies are over all Your works.

147:3-6 You heal the brokenhearted and bind up my wounds. You count the number of the stars; You call them all by name. Great are You, Lord, and mighty in power; Your understanding is infinite. Lord, You lift up the humble; You cast the wicked down to the ground.

145:15-20 My eyes look expectantly to You, and You give me my food in due season. You open Your hand and satisfy the desire of every living thing. Lord, You are righteous in all Your ways, gracious in all Your works. Lord, You are near to all who call upon You, to all who call upon You in truth. You will fulfill the desire of those who fear You; You also will hear my cry and save me. Lord, You preserve all who love You, but all the wicked You will destroy.

149:4 For You, Lord, take pleasure in Your people; You will beautify the humble with salvation.

Chapter 5

A.C.C.T.S.

THANKSGIVING

5:3 My voice You shall hear in the morning, O Lord; in the morning I will direct it to You, and I will look up.

5:7 But as for me, I will come into Your house in the multitude of Your mercy; in fear of You I will worship toward Your holy temple.

5:11 But I shall rejoice in You and put my trust in You; let me ever shout for joy, because You defend me; let me also love Your name and be joyful in You.

7:17 I will praise You, Lord, according to Your righteousness, and will sing praise to Your name my Lord Most High.

8:1 O Lord, my Lord how excellent is Your name in all the earth. Who have set Your glory above the heavens.

9:1 O Lord, my Lord, How excellent is Your name in all the earth, Who have set Your glory above the heavens!

13:5-6 But I have trusted in Your mercy; my heart shall rejoice in Your salvation. I will sing to You, Lord, because You have dealt bountifully with me.

16:7 I will bless You, Lord, who has given me counsel; my heart also instructs me in the night seasons.

18:1-3 I will love You, O Lord, my strength. You, Lord, are my rock and my fortress and my deliverer; my God, my strength, in whom I will trust; my shield and the horn of my salvation, my stronghold. I will call upon You, Lord, who is worthy to be praised; so shall I be saved from my enemies.

18:19 You also brought me out into a broad place; You delivered me because You delighted in me.

18:46 Lord You live! Blessed be my Rock! Let the God of my salvation be exalted.

21:13 Be exalted, O Lord, in Your own strength! I will sing and praise Your power.

22:22 I will declare Your name to my brethren; in the midst of the assembly I will praise You.

22:26-29 The poor shall eat and be satisfied; those of us who seek You will praise You, Lord. Let my heart live forever! All the ends of the world shall remember and turn to You, Lord, and all the families of the nations shall worship before You. For the kingdom is Yours Lord, and You rule over the nations. All the prosperous of the earth shall eat and worship; all those who go down to the dust shall bow before You, even he who cannot keep himself alive.

26:7-8 That I may proclaim with the voice of thanksgiving, and tell of all Your wondrous works. Lord, I have loved the habitation of Your house, and the place where Your glory dwells.

26:11-12 But as for me, I will walk in my integrity; redeem me and be merciful to me. My foot stands in an even place; in the congregations I will bless You, Lord.

27:1 Lord, You are my light and my salvation; whom shall I fear? You, Lord are the strength of my life; of whom shall I be afraid?

27:6 And now my head shall be lifted up above my enemies all around me; therefore I will offer sacrifices of joy in Your tabernacle; I will sing, yes, I will sing praises to You, Lord.

28:6 Blessed are You, Lord, because You have heard the voice of my supplications! Lord, You are my strength and my shield; my heart trusts in You, and I am helped; therefore my heart greatly rejoices, and with my song I will praise You.

29:1-2 Give unto the Lord, O you mighty ones. I will give unto the Lord glory and strength. I will give unto the Lord the glory due to Your name; I will worship You, Lord, in the beauty of Your holiness.

30:1 I will extol You, O Lord, for You have lifted me up, and have not let my foes rejoice over me.

30:4 I shall sing praise to You, Lord, for I am Your saint, and I give thanks at the remembrance of Your Holy Name.

30:12 To the end that my glory may sing praise to You and not be silent. O Lord my God, I will give thanks to You forever.

31:19 Oh, how great is Your goodness, which You have laid up for those who fear You, which You have prepared for those who trust in You, in the presence of the sons of men!

31:21 Blessed be You, Lord, for You have shown me Your marvelous kindness in a strong city!

32:11 I will be glad in You, Lord,

and rejoice in Your righteousness; and shout for joy, with all those who are upright in heart!

33:1-3 I will rejoice in You, Lord, we who are righteous! For praise from the upright is beautiful. I will praise You, Lord, with the harp; I will make a melody to You with an instrument of ten strings. I will sing to You a new song and play skillfully with a shout of joy.

34:1-3 I will bless You, Lord, at all times; Your praise shall continually be in my mouth. My soul shall make its boast in You, Lord; the humble shall hear of it and be glad. Oh, I magnify You, Lord, and exalt Your name with others.

37:3-5 I will trust in You, Lord, and do good; dwell in the land, and feed on Your faithfulness. I will delight in You, Lord, and You shall give me the desires of my heart. I shall commit my ways to You, Lord, and trust also in You, and You shall bring it to pass.

37:7 I will rest in You, Lord, and wait patiently for You; I will not fret because of You who prospers me in Your way.

37:11 But the meek shall inherit the earth, and shall delight ourselves in the abundance of Your peace.

43:4-5 I will go to Your altar God, for You are my exceeding joy; and on the harp I will praise You, O God, my God. Why are you cast down, O my soul? And why are you disquieted within me? I will hope in You God; for I shall yet praise You.

47:-21 Oh, clap your hands, all you peoples! Shout to God with the voice of triumph! For You, Lord, Most High are awesome; You are a great King over all the earth.

47:5-9 God, You have gone up with a shout, Lord with the sound of a trumpet. We shall sing praises to You God, sing praises! Sing praises to You my King, sing praises! For You God, are the King of all the earth; I will sing praises with understanding. God, You reign over the nations; You are God who sits on Your holy throne. The princes of the people have gathered together, Your people, O God of Abraham. For the shields of the earth belong to You God; You are greatly exalted.

48:1 Great are You, Lord, and greatly to be praised in Your City, God, in Your holy mountain.

50:4-6 You shall call to the heavens from above, and to the earth, that You may judge Your people: "Gather My saints together to Me, those who have made a covenant with Me by sacrifice." Let the heavens declare Your righteousness, for God, You yourself are the Judge.

50:23 Whoever offers praise glorifies You; and to him who orders his conduct aright You will show Your salvation, God."

52:9 I will praise You forever, because You have done it; and in the presence of Your saints, I will wait on Your name, for it is good.

57:5 Be exalted, O God, above the heavens; let Your glory be above all the earth.

57:7-11 My heart is steadfast, O God, my heart is steadfast; I will sing and give You praise. Awake, my glory! Awake, lute and harp! I will awaken the dawn. I will praise You, O Lord, among the people; I will sing to You among the nations. For Your mercy reaches unto the heavens, and Your truth unto the clouds. Be exalted, O God, above the heavens; let Your glory be above all the earth.

63:3-5 Because Your lovingkindness is better than life, my lips shall praise You. Thus I will bless You while I live; I will lift up my hands in Your name. My soul shall be satisfied as with marrow and fatness, and my mouth shall praise You with joyful lips.

63:7-8 Because You have been my help, therefore in the shadow of Your wings I will rejoice. My soul follows close behind You; Your right hand upholds me.

64:9-10 All men shall fear, and shall declare Your works God; for they shall wisely consider Your doing. The righteous shall be glad in You, Lord, and trust in You. And all the upright in heart shall glory.

65:1-2 Praise is awaiting You, O God, in Zion; and to You the vow shall be performed. O You who hear prayer, to You all flesh will come.

65:5-8 By awesome deeds in righteousness You will answer me, O God of my salvation, You who are the confidence of all the ends of the earth, and of the far-off seas; who established the mountains by Your strength, being clothed with power; You who still the noise of the seas, the noise of their waves, and the tumult of the people. They also who dwell in the farthest parts are afraid of Your signs; You make the out goings of the morning and evening rejoice.

65:11 You crown the year with Your goodness, and Your paths drip with abundance.

66:1-5 Make a joyful shout to God, all the earth! Sing out the honor of Your name; make Your praise glorious. Say to God, "How awesome are Your works! Through the greatness of Your power Your enemies shall submit themselves to You. All the earth shall worship You And sing praises to You; they shall sing praises to Your name." Come and see the works of God; You are awesome in Your doing toward the sons of men.

66:8-9 Oh, bless our God, you people! And make the voice of your praise to be heard, who keeps our soul among the living, and does not allow our feet to be moved.

66:20 Blessed be to You, God, You have not turned away my prayer, nor Your mercy from me!

68:3-4 But let the righteous be glad; let us rejoice before You, God; yes, let us rejoice exceedingly. We sing to You God, sing praises to Your name; extol You who rides on the clouds, by Your name YAHWEY, and rejoice before You.

68:19-20 Blessed be to You, Lord, who daily loads me with benefits, You are the God of my salvation! You are the God of salvation; and to You GOD, my Lord, belong escapes from death.

68:32-33 I sing to You God, as part of your kingdom of the earth; oh, I sing praises to You, Lord, to You who rides on the heaven of heavens, which were of old! Indeed, You send out Your voice, a mighty voice.

68:35 O God, You are more awesome than Your holy places. The God of Israel is You who gives strength and power to Your people.

70:4 Let all those who seek You rejoice and be glad in You; and let those who love Your salvation say continually, "Let God be magnified!"

71:8 Let my mouth be filled with Your praise and with Your glory all the day.

71:22-23 Also with the lute I will praise You and Your faithfulness, O my God! To You I will sing with the harp, O Holy One of Israel. My lips shall greatly rejoice when I sing to You, and my soul, which You have redeemed.

72:17-19 Your name shall endure forever; Your name shall continue as long as the sun. And men shall be blessed in You; all nations shall call You blessed. Blessed be You, Lord, God, the God of Israel. Who only does wondrous things! And blessed be Your glorious name forever! And let the whole earth be filled with Your glory. Amen and Amen.

73:23-26 Nevertheless You are continually with me; You hold me by Your right hand. You will guide me with Your counsel, and afterward receive me to glory. Whom have I in heaven but You? And there is none upon earth that I desire besides You. My flesh and my heart fail; but God, You are the strength of my heart and my portion forever.

73:28 But it is good for me to draw near to You God; I have put my trust in You, Lord, GOD, that I may declare all Your works.

74:21 Oh, do not let the oppressed return ashamed! Let the poor and needy praise Your name.

75:1, 9 I give thanks to You, O God, I give thanks! For Your wondrous works declare that Your name is near. But I will declare forever, I will sing praises to the God of Jacob.

76:4 You are more glorious and excellent than the mountains of prey.

77:12-15 I will also meditate on all Your work, and talk of Your deeds. Your way, O God, is in the sanctuary; who is so great a God as You my God? You are the God who does wonders; You have declared Your strength among the people. You have with Your arm redeemed me, one of your people.

78:7-8 That I may set my hope in You God, and not forget Your works, but keep Your commandments; and may I not be like my father, stubborn and rebellious. Like those before me in a generation that did not set its heart aright, and whose spirit was not faithful to God.

79:13 So I am, Your people and a sheep of Your pasture. I will give You thanks forever; I will show forth Your praise to all generations.

81:1 I will sing aloud to You God of my strength; I will make a joyful shout to You, God of Jacob.

84:1-4, 8 How lovely is Your tabernacle, O Lord of hosts! My soul longs, yes, even faints for Your courts, Lord; my heart and my flesh cry out for You, the living God. Even the sparrow has found a home, and the swallow a nest for herself, where she may lay her young—Even Your altars, O Lord of hosts, my King and my God. Blessed are those who dwell in Your house; they will still be praising You. Give ear, O God of Jacob!

84:9-10 O God, behold You are my shield, look upon the face of Your anointed. For a day in Your courts is better than a thousand. I would rather be a doorkeeper in the house of my God than dwell in the tents of wickedness.

86:11-13 Teach me Your way, O Lord; I will walk in Your truth; unite my heart to fear Your name. I will praise You, O Lord my God, with all my heart, and I will glorify Your name forevermore. For great is Your mercy toward me, and You have delivered my soul from the depths of Sheol.

89:1-2 I will sing of Your mercies Lord forever; with my mouth will I make known Your faithfulness to all generations. For I have said, "Mercy shall be built up forever; Your faithfulness You shall establish in the very heavens."

89:5-8 And the heavens will praise Your wonders, O Lord; Your faithfulness also in the assembly of the saints. For who in the heavens can be compared to You, Lord? Who among the sons of the mighty can be likened to You, Lord? God, You are greatly to be feared in the assembly of the saints, and to be held in reverence by all those around You. O Lord, God of hosts, Who is mighty like You, O Lord? Your faithfulness also surrounds You.

89:15-18 Blessed are the people who know the joyful sound! We walk, O Lord, in the light of Your countenance. In Your name I rejoice all day long, and in Your righteousness I will be exalted. For You are the glory of my strength, and in Your favor my horn is exalted. For my shield belongs to You, Lord, and my King to the Holy One of Israel.

89:26 I shall cry to You, 'You are my Father, My God, and the rock of my salvation.'

90:1-2, 4 Lord, You have been my dwelling place, and will be for all generations. Before the mountains were brought forth, or ever You had formed the earth and the world, Even from everlasting to everlasting, You are God. For a thousand years in Your sight are like yesterday when it is past, and like a watch in the night.

90:16-17 Let Your work appear to Your servants, and Your glory to my children. And let Your beauty Lord, God be upon me, and establish the work of my hands for You; yes, establish the work of my hands.

92:1-2 It is good to give thanks to You, Lord, and to sing praises to Your name, O Most High; to declare Your lovingkindness in the morning, and Your faithfulness every night.

92:13-15 Those who are planted in the house of the Lord shall flourish in Your courts O God. I shall still bear fruit in old age; I shall be fresh and flourishing and declare that You, Lord, are upright; You are my rock, and there is no unrighteousness in You.

93:1-2 Lord, You reign, You are clothed with majesty; You have girded Yourself with strength. Surely the world is established, so that it cannot be moved. Your throne is established from of old; You are from everlasting.

94:12-14 Blessed is the man whom You instruct, O Lord, and teach out of Your law. That You may give me rest from the days of adversity, until the pit is dug for the wicked. For You, Lord, will not cast off Your people, nor will You forsake Your inheritance.

94:17-19 Lord, unless You had been my help, my soul would soon have settled in silence. If I say, "My foot slips," Your mercy, O Lord, will hold me up. In the multitude of my anxieties within me, Your comforts delight my soul.

95:1-11 Oh come, I shall sing to You, Lord! I shall shout joyfully to You, the Rock of my salvation. I shall come before Your presence with thanksgiving; I shall shout joyfully to You with psalms. For You, Lord, are the great God, and the great King above all gods. In Your hand are the deep places of the earth; the heights of the hills are Yours also. The sea is Yours, for You made it; and Your hands formed the dry land. Oh come, let me worship and bow down; let me kneel before You, Lord, my Maker. For You are my God, and I am one of your sheep of Your pasture, and the sheep of Your hand. Today, I will hear Your voice: "Do not harden your heart, as in the rebellion, as in the day of trial in the wilderness, when your fathers tested Me; they tried Me, though they saw My work. For forty years I was grieved with that generation, and said, 'It is a people who go astray in their hearts, and they do not know My ways.' So I swore in My wrath, 'They shall not enter My rest.'"

96:1-13 Oh, I sing to You, Lord a new song! I will sing to You, Lord, and all the earth. I will sing to You, Lord, and bless Your name; I will proclaim the good news of Your salvation from day to day. I will declare Your glory among the nations, Your wonders among all peoples. For You, Lord, are great and greatly to be praised; You are to be feared above all gods. For all the gods of the peoples are idols, but You, Lord, made the heavens. I will give you honor. Majesty is before You; strength and beauty are in Your sanctuary. I will give to You, Lord, glory and strength.

I will give to You, Lord, the glory due Your name; I will bring an offering, and come into Your courts. Oh, I love to worship You, Lord, in Your beauty of holiness! I tremble before You, as should all the earth. I will say among the nations, "The Lord reigns; the world also is firmly established, it shall not be moved; You shall judge the peoples righteously." Let the heavens rejoice, and let the earth be glad; let the sea roar, and all its fullness; let the field be joyful, and all that is in it. Then all the trees of the woods will rejoice before You, Lord. For You are coming, for You are coming to judge the earth. You shall judge the world with righteousness, and the people with Your truth.

97:1 Lord, You reign; let the earth rejoice; let the multitude of isles be glad!

97:6 The heavens declare Your righteousness, and all the people see Your glory.

97:9-12 For You, Lord, are most high above all the earth; You are exalted far above all gods. Because I love You, Lord, I too hate evil! You preserve the souls of Your saints; You deliver them out of the hand of the wicked. Light is sown for the righteous, and gladness for the upright in heart. I will rejoice in You, Lord, for You are righteous, and I give thanks at the remembrance of Your holy name.

98:1 Oh, I shall sing to You, Lord, a new song! For You have done marvelous things; Your right hand and Your holy arm have gained Your victory.

98:4 I shall shout joyfully to You, Lord, with all the earth; breaking forth in song, rejoicing, and singing praises.

99:3 Let me praise Your great and awesome name—You are holy.

99:5 I exalt You, Lord, my God, and worship at Your footstool— You are holy

99:8-9 You answered me, O Lord my God; You are to me 'God-Who-Forgives,' though You took vengeance on my deeds. I exalt You, Lord, my God, and worship at Your holy hill; for You, Lord, my God are holy.

100:1-5 I will make a joyful shout to You, Lord, all you lands! I will serve You, Lord, with gladness; I come before Your presence with singing. I know that You, Lord, You are God; it is You who has made me, and not myself; I am Your child and the sheep of Your pasture. I enter into Your gates with thanksgiving, and into Your courts with praise. I am thankful to You, and bless Your name. For Lord, You are good; Your mercy is everlasting, and Your truth endures to all generations.

101:1 I will sing of Your mercy and justice; to You, O Lord, I will sing praises.

102:27 You are the same, and Your years will have no end.

103:1-5 Bless You, Lord, O my soul; and all that is within me, bless Your holy name! Bless You, Lord, O my soul, and forget not all Your benefits: Who forgives all my iniquities, who heals all my diseases, who redeems my life from destruction, who crowns me with lovingkindness and tender mercies, Who satisfies my mouth with good things, so that my youth is renewed like the eagle's.

103:8 Lord, You are merciful and gracious, slow to anger, and abounding in mercy.

104:1-4 Bless You, Lord, O my soul! O Lord my God, You are very great: You are clothed with honor and majesty, You cover Yourself with light as with a garment, You stretch out the heavens like a curtain. You lay the beams of Your upper chambers in the waters, You make the clouds Your chariot, You walk on the wings of the wind, You make Your angels spirits, Your ministers a flame of fire.

104:31 May Your glory, Lord, endure forever; may I rejoice in Your works, Lord.

104:33-34 I will sing to You, Lord, as long as I live; I will sing praise to You, my God, while I have my being. May my meditation be sweet to You; I will be glad in You, Lord.

105:1-5 Oh, I give thanks to You, Lord! I call upon Your name; make known Your deeds among Your people! I will sing to You, sing psalms to You; I will talk of all Your wondrous works! Glory in Your holy name; let my heart rejoice with those who seek You, Lord! I will seek You, Lord, and Your strength; I will seek Your face evermore! I remember Your marvelous works, which You have done.

106:1-3 Praise You, Lord! Oh, I give thanks to You, Lord, for You are good! For Your mercy endures forever. Who can utter the mighty acts of You, Lord? Who can declare all Your praise? Blessed are those who keep justice, and those who do righteousness at all times!

106:47-48 Save me, O Lord my God, and gather me from among the Gentiles, to give thanks to Your holy name, to triumph in Your praise. Blessed be to You, Lord, God of Israel from everlasting to everlasting! And let all the people say, "Amen!" Praise You, Lord!

107:1 Oh, I give thanks to You, Lord, for You are good! For Your mercy endures forever.

107:31-32 Oh, that men would give thanks to You, Lord, for Your goodness, and for Your wonderful works to the children of men! Let us exalt You also in the assembly of the people, and praise You in the company of the elders.

108:1-5 O God, my heart is steadfast; I will sing and give praise, even with my glory. Awake, lute and harp! I will awaken the dawn. I will praise You, O Lord, among the people, and I will sing praises to You among the nations. For Your mercy is great above the heavens, and Your truth reaches to the clouds. Be exalted, O God, above the heavens, and Your glory above all the earth.

109:30-31 I will greatly praise You, Lord, with my mouth; yes, I will praise You among the multitude. For You shall stand at the right hand of the poor, to save me from those who condemn me.

111:1 Praise You, Lord! I will praise You, Lord, with my whole heart, in the assembly of the upright and in the congregation.

111:4 You have made Your wonderful works to be remembered; Lord, You are gracious and full of compassion.

112:1 Praise You, Lord! Blessed is the man who fears You, Lord, who delights greatly in Your commandments.

113:1-3 Praise You, Lord! Praise, O servants of the Lord, praise Your name O Lord! Blessed be Your name Lord from this time forth and forevermore! From the rising of the sun to its going down. Your name Lord, is to be praised.

113:4-6 Lord, You are high above all nations, Your glory above the heavens. Who is like You, Lord, my God? Who dwells on high, who humbles Himself to behold the things that are in the heavens and in the earth?

116:17-19 I will offer to You the sacrifice of thanksgiving, and will call upon Your name Lord. I will pay my vows to You, Lord, now in the presence of all Your people, in the courts of Your house, in the midst of Jerusalem. I will praise You, Lord!

117:1-2 I Praise You, Lord! I exalt You, with all Your people! For Your merciful kindness is great toward me, and the truth of You, Lord, endures forever. Praise You, Lord!

118:1 Oh, I give thanks to You, Lord, for You are good! For Your mercy endures forever.

118:24 This is the day Lord, You have made; I will rejoice and be glad in it.

118:28-29 You are my God, and I will praise You; You are my God, I will exalt You. Oh, I give thanks to You, Lord, for You are good! For Your mercy endures forever.

119:12 Blessed are You, O Lord! Teach me Your statutes.

121:1-2 I will lift up my eyes to the hills—from whence comes my help? My help comes from You, Lord, who made heaven and earth.

123:1-2 Unto You I lift up my eyes, O You who dwell in the heavens. Behold, as the eyes of servants look to the hand of their masters, As the eyes of a maid to the hand of her mistress, so my eyes look to You, Lord, my God, until You have mercy on me.

124:8 My help is in Your name Lord, who made heaven and earth.

134:1-3 Behold, I will bless You, Lord, with all you servants Lord, who by night stand in Your house! I lift up my hands in the sanctuary, and bless You, Lord. To You, Lord, who made heaven and earth. Bless you from Zion!

135:1-3 Praise You, Lord! Praise Your name Lord; I praise You, I am Your servant Lord! I stand in Your house Lord, in the courts of Your house my God. Praise You, Lord, for You are good; I sing praises to Your name, for it is pleasant.

135:5 For I know that You, Lord, are great, and You, Lord, are above all gods.

135:13 Your name, O Lord, endures forever, Your fame, O Lord, throughout all generations.

135:20 Bless You, Lord! I fear Your name Lord, I will bless You!

136:1-3 Oh, I give thanks to You, Lord, for You are good! For Your mercy endures forever. Oh, I give thanks to You, God of gods! For Your mercy endures forever. Oh, I give thanks to You, Lord of Lords! For Your mercy endures forever.

136:26 Oh, I give thanks to You God of heaven! For Your mercy endures forever.

138:1-2 I will praise You with my whole heart; before the gods I will sing praises to You. I will worship toward Your holy temple, and praise Your name for Your lovingkindness and Your truth; for You have magnified Your word above all is Your name.

138:4-5 All the kings of the earth shall praise You, O Lord, when they hear the words of Your mouth. Yes, they shall sing of the ways of the Lord, for great is Your glory Lord.

139:14 I will praise You, for I am fearfully and wonderfully made; marvelous are Your works, and that my soul knows very well.

143:8 Cause me to hear Your lovingkindness in the morning, for in You do I trust; cause me to know the way in which I should walk, for I lift up my soul to You.

144:1 Blessed are You, Lord, my Rock.

144:5 I bow down to Your heavens, O Lord, come down; touch the mountains, and they shall smoke.

144:9 I will sing a new song to You, O God; on a harp of ten strings I will sing praises to You.

144:15 Happy are the people who are in such a state; happy are the people whose God is You, Lord!

145:1-7 I will extol You, my God, O King; and I will bless Your name forever and ever. Every day I will bless You, and I will praise Your name forever and ever. Great are You, Lord, and greatly to be praised; and Your greatness is unsearchable. One generation shall praise Your works to another, and shall declare Your mighty acts. I will meditate on the glorious splendor of Your majesty,

and on Your wondrous works. Men shall speak of the might of Your awesome acts, and I will declare Your greatness. They shall utter the memory of Your great goodness, and shall sing of Your righteousness.

145:10-11 All Your works shall praise You, O Lord, and Your saints shall bless You. I shall speak of the glory of Your kingdom, and talk of Your power.

145:14 Lord, You uphold all who fall, and raise up all who are bowed down.

146:1 Praise You, Lord! Praise You, Lord, O my soul! While I live I will praise You, Lord; I will sing praises to You my God while I have my being.

146:10 Lord, You shall reign forever—You God, O Zion, to all generations. We praise You, Lord!

147:1 Praise You, Lord! For it is good to sing praises to You God; for it is pleasant, and praise is beautiful.

147:12 Praise You, Lord, O Jerusalem! Praise You my God, O Zion!

148:1-6 Praise You, Lord! Praise You, Lord, from the heavens; Praise You in the heights! Praise You, all Your angels; Praise You, all Your hosts! Praise You, sun and moon; Praise You, all you stars of light! Praise You, heavens of heavens, and you waters above the heavens! Let us praise Your name Lord, for You commanded and they were created. You also established them forever and ever; You made a decree which shall not pass away.

148:13 Let me praise Your name Lord, for Your name alone is exalted; Your glory is above the earth and heaven.

149:1-2 Praise You, Lord! I sing to You, Lord, a new song, and praise You in the assembly of saints. Let me praise Your name with the dance; let me sing praises to You with the timbrel and harp.

149:5-6 Let Your saints be joyful in glory; let me sing aloud on my bed. Let Your high praises, God be in my mouth,

150:1-6 Praise You, Lord! Praise You God, in Your sanctuary; Praise You in Your mighty firmament! Praise You for Your mighty acts; Praise You according to Your excellent greatness! Praise You with the sound of the trumpet; Praise You with the lute and harp! Praise You with the timbrel and dance; Praise You with stringed instruments and flutes! Praise You with loud cymbals; Praise You with clashing cymbals! Let everything

that has breath praise You, Lord. I praise You, Lord!

Chapter 6

A.C.C.T.S.

SUPPLICATION

4:1 Hear me when I call You, O God of my righteousness! You have relieved me in my distress; have mercy on me, and hear my prayer.

5:1-3 Give ear to my words, O Lord, Consider my meditation. Give heed to the voice of my cry, my King and my God, for to You I will pray. My voice You shall hear in the morning, O Lord; in the morning I will direct it to You, and I will look up.

5:8 Lead me O Lord, in Your righteousness because of my enemies. Make Your way straight before my face.

6:1-5 O Lord, do not rebuke me in Your anger, nor chasten me in Your hot displeasure. Have mercy on me, O Lord, for I am weak; O Lord, heal me, for my bones are troubled. My soul also is greatly troubled; O Lord—how long? Return, O Lord, deliver me! Save me for Your mercies' sake! For in death there is no remembrance of You; in the grave who will give You thanks?

6:6 I am weary with my groaning; night I make my bed swim; I drench my couch with my tears. My eye wastes away because of grief; I grow old because of all my enemies.

6:8 For You, Lord, have heard the voice of my weeping. Lord hear my supplication; Lord receive my prayer.

7:1-2 O Lord my God, in You I put my trust; save me from all those who persecute me; and deliver me, lest they tear me like a lion, rending me in pieces, while there is none to deliver.

9:13 Have mercy on me, O Lord! Consider my trouble from those who hate me, You who lift me up from the gates of death,

10:1 Why do You stand afar off, O Lord? Why do You hide in times of trouble?

10:12 Arise, O Lord! O God, lift up Your hand! Do not forget me, I humble myself before you.

12:1 Help, Lord, for the godly man ceases!

13:1 How long, O Lord? Will You forget me forever? How long will

You hide Your face from me?

13:2 How long shall I take counsel in my soul, having sorrow in my heart daily? How long will my enemy be exalted over me?

13:3 Consider and hear me, O Lord my God; enlighten my eyes,

17:1 Hear a just cause, O Lord, attend to my cry; give ear to my prayer which is not from deceitful lips.

17:6 I have called upon You, for You will hear me, O God; incline Your ear to me, and hear my speech.

17:13 Arise, O Lord, confront him, cast him down; deliver my life from the wicked with Your sword.

22:1-5 My God, my God, why have You forsaken me? Why are You so far from helping me, and from the words of my groaning? O my God, I cry in the daytime, but You do not hear; And in the night season, I am not silent. But You are holy, enthroned in the praises of Israel. Our fathers trusted in You; they trusted, and You delivered them. They cried to You, and were delivered; they trusted in You, and were not ashamed.

25:20-21 Keep my soul, and deliver me; let me not be ashamed, for I put my trust in You. Let integrity and uprightness preserve me. I

shall continue to wait for You.

27:7-10 Hear, O Lord, when I cry with my voice! Have mercy also upon me, and answer me. When You said, "Seek My face," My heart says to You, "Your face, Lord, I will seek." Do not hide Your face from me; do not turn Your servant away in anger; You have been my help; do not leave me nor forsake me, O God of my salvation. When my father and my mother forsake me, then You, Lord, will take care of me.

28:1-2 To You I will cry, O Lord my Rock: Do not be silent to me, lest, if You are silent to me, I become like those who go down to the pit. Hear the voice of my supplications when I cry to You, when I lift up my hands toward Your holy sanctuary.

31:1-2 In You, O Lord, I put my trust; let me never be ashamed; deliver me in Your righteousness. Bow down Your ear to me, deliver me speedily; be my rock of refuge, a fortress of defense to save me.

31:9-10 Have mercy on me, O Lord, for I am in trouble; my eye wastes away with grief, yes, my soul and my body! For my life is spent with grief, and my years with sighing; my strength fails because of my iniquity, and my bones waste away.

31:21-22 Blessed are You, Lord, for You have shown me Your marvelous kindness in a strong city! For I said in my haste, "I am cut off from before Your eyes"; nevertheless You heard the voice of my supplications when I cried out to You.

34:4, 6-9 I sought You, Lord, and You heard me, and delivered me from all my fears. I cried out, and You, Lord, heard me, and saved me out of all my troubles. The angel of the Lord encamps all around those who fear Him, and delivers us. Oh, I taste and see that You, Lord, are good; blessed is the man or women who trusts in You! Oh, how I fear You, Lord, as one of Your saints!

34:15-16 Your eyes Lord, are on the righteous, and Your ears are open to their cry. Your face Lord is against those who do evil, You will cut off the remembrance of them from the earth.

34:17 The righteous cry out, and You, Lord, hear, and You deliver me out of all my troubles.

35:1-3 I plead my cause with you, O Lord, with those who strive with me; fight against those who fight against me. Take hold of shield and buckler, and stand up for my help. Also draw out the spear, and stop those who pursue me. You say to my soul, "I am your salvation."

35:10 All my bones shall say, 'Lord, who is like You, delivering the poor from those who is too strong for him, yes, the poor and the needy from those who plunder us?'

35:22-24 This You have seen, O Lord; do not keep silent. O Lord, do not be far from me. Stir up Yourself, and awake to my vindication, to my cause, my God and my Lord. Vindicate me, O Lord my God, according to Your righteousness.

37:39-40 But the salvation of the righteous is from You, Lord; You are my strength in the time of trouble. And You, Lord, shall help and deliver me; You shall deliver me from the wicked, and save me, because I trust in You.

38:11-12 My loved ones and my friends stand aloof from my plague, and my relatives stand afar off. Those also who seek my life lay snares for me; those who seek my hurt speak of destruction, and plan deception all the day long.

38:15, 21-22 For in You, O Lord, I hope; You will hear, O Lord my God. Do not forsake me, O Lord; O my God, be not far from me! Make haste to help me, O Lord, my salvation!

40:13 Be pleased, O Lord, to deliver me; O Lord, make haste to help me!

40:17 But I am poor and needy; yet You, Lord, think about me. You are my help and my deliverer; do not delay, O my God.

42:9, 11 I will say to You God, my Rock, "Why have You forgotten me? Why do I go mourning because of the oppression of the enemy?" Why am I cast down, O my soul? And why am I disquieted within me? I hope in You God; for I shall yet praise You, the help of my countenance and my God.

43:1-3 Vindicate me, O God, and plead my cause against an ungodly nation; oh, deliver me from the deceitful and unjust man! For You are the God of my strength; why do You cast me off? Why do I go mourning because of the oppression of the enemy? Oh, send out Your light and Your truth! Let them lead me; let them bring me to Your holy hill and to Your tabernacle.

44:23-26 Awake! Why do You sleep, O Lord? Arise! Do not cast me off forever. Why do You hide Your face, and forget my affliction and my oppression? For my soul is bowed down to the dust; my body clings to the ground. Arise and help me, and redeem me for Your mercies' sake.

51:7-8 Purge me with hyssop, and I shall be clean; wash me, and I shall be whiter than snow. Make me hear joy and gladness, that the bones You have broken may rejoice.

54:1-3 Save me, O God, by Your name, and vindicate me by Your strength. Hear my prayer, O God; give ear to the words of my mouth. For strangers have risen up against me, and oppressors have sought after my life; they have not set You God before them.

55:1 Give ear to my prayer, O God, and do not hide Yourself from my supplication.

55:4 My heart is severely pained within me, and the terrors of death have fallen upon me.

55:22 I will cast my burdens on You, Lord, and You shall sustain me; You shall never permit the righteous to be moved.

57:1-3 Be merciful to me, O God, be merciful to me! For my soul trusts in You; and in the shadow of Your wings I will make my refuge until these calamities have passed by. I will cry out to You my God ,Most High, to You who performs all things for me. You shall send from heaven and save me; You reproach the one who would swallow me up.

59:1 Deliver me from my enemies, O my God; defend me from those who rise up against me.

60:11-12 Give me help from trouble, for the help of man is useless. Through You, God, I will do valiantly, for it is You who shall tread down my enemies.

61:1-3 Hear my cry, O God; attend to my prayer. From the end of the earth I will cry to You, when my heart is overwhelmed; lead me to the rock that is higher than I. For You have been a shelter for me, a strong tower from the enemy.

64:1 Hear my voice, O God, in my meditation; preserve my life from fear of the enemy.

67:1 God be merciful to me and bless me, and cause Your face to shine upon me.

69:1-3 Save me, O God! For the waters have come up to my neck. I sink in deep mire, where there is no standing; I have come into deep waters, where the floods overflow me. I am weary with my crying; my throat is dry; my eyes fail while I wait for You, my God.

69:16-18, 20 Hear me, O Lord, for Your lovingkindness is good; turn to me according to the multitude of Your tender mercies. And do not hide Your face from Your servant, for I am in trouble; hear me speedily. Draw near to my soul, and redeem it; deliver me because of my enemies. Reproach has broken my heart, and I am full of heaviness; I looked for someone to take pity, but there was none; and for comforters, but I found none.

69:32 I shall seek You, God, my heart shall live for You, Lord, hear the poor.

70:1 Make haste, O God, to deliver me! Make haste to help me, O Lord!

70:5 But I am poor and needy; make haste to me, O God! You are my help and my deliverer; O Lord, do not delay.

71:1-6 In You, O Lord, I put my trust; let me never be put to shame. Deliver me in Your righteousness, and cause me to escape; incline Your ear to me, and save me. Be my strong refuge, to which I may resort continually; You have given the commandment to save me, for You are my rock and my fortress. For You are my hope, O Lord GOD; You are my trust from my youth. By You I have been upheld from birth; You are He who took me out of my mother's womb. My praise shall be continually of You.

71:9 Do not cast me off in the time of old age; do not forsake me when my strength fails.

71:12 O God, do not be far from me; O my God, make haste to help me!

72:12-14 For You will deliver the needy when we cry, the poor also, and to those of us who have no helper. You will spare the poor and needy, and will save the souls of the needy. You will redeem my life from oppression and violence; and precious shall be my blood in Your sight.

77:1-3 I cried out to You, God, with my voice; and You gave ear to me. In the day of my trouble I sought You, Lord; my hand was stretched out in the night without ceasing; my soul refused to be comforted. I remembered God, and was troubled; I complained, and my spirit was overwhelmed.

77:4-6 You hold my eyelids open; I am so troubled that I cannot speak. I have considered the days of old, The years of ancient times. I call to remembrance my song in the night; I meditate within my heart, and my spirit makes a diligent search.

79:8-9 Oh, do not remember former iniquities against me! Let Your tender mercies come speedily to meet me, for I have been brought very low. Help me, O God of my salvation, for the glory of Your name; and deliver me, and

provide atonement for my sins, for Your name's sake!

80:3 Restore me, O God; cause Your face to shine, and I shall be saved!

85:4-7 Restore me, O God of my salvation, and cause Your anger toward me to cease. Will You be angry with me forever? Will You prolong Your anger to all generations? Will You not revive me again, that I may rejoice in You? Show me Your mercy, Lord, and grant me Your salvation.

86:1-6 Bow down Your ear, O Lord, hear me; preserve my life, for I am holy; You are my God; save Your servant who trusts in You! Be merciful to me, O Lord, for I cry to You all day long. Rejoice the soul of Your servant, for to You, O Lord, I lift up my soul. For You, Lord, are good, and ready to forgive, and abundant in mercy to all those who call upon You. Give ear, O Lord, to my prayer; and attend to the voice of my supplications. In the day of my trouble I will call upon You, for You will answer me.

88:1-12 O Lord, God of my salvation, I have cried out day and night before You. Let my prayer come before You; incline Your ear to my cry. For my soul is full of troubles, and my life draws near to the grave. I am counted with those who go down to the pit; I am like a man who has no strength, adrift among the dead, Like the slain who lie in the grave, whom You remember no more, and who are cut off from Your hand. You have laid me in the lowest pit, in darkness, in the depths. Your wrath lies heavy upon me, and You have afflicted me with all Your waves. You have put away my acquaintances far from me; You have made me an abomination to them; I am shut up, and I cannot get out; my eye wastes away because of affliction. Lord, I have called daily upon You; I have stretched out my hands to You. Will You work wonders for the dead? Shall the dead arise and praise You? Shall Your lovingkindness be declared in the grave? Or Your faithfulness in the place of destruction? Shall Your wonders be known in the dark? And Your righteousness in the land of forgetfulness?

102:1-2 Hear my prayer, O Lord, and let my cry come to You. Do not hide Your face from me in the day of my trouble; incline Your ear to me; in the day that I call, answer me speedily.

106:4-5 Remember me, O Lord, with the favor You have toward Your people. Oh, visit me with Your salvation, that I may see the benefit of Your chosen ones, that I

may rejoice in the gladness of Your nation, that I may glory with Your inheritance.

107:6 Then I cried out to You, Lord, in my trouble, and You delivered me out of my distresses.

107:13-15, 28 Then I cried out to You, Lord, in my trouble, and You saved me out of my distresses. You brought me out of darkness and the shadow of death, and broke my chains in pieces. Oh, that men would give thanks to You, Lord, for Your goodness, and for Your wonderful works to the children of men! Then they cry out to You, Lord, in their trouble, and You bring them out of their distresses.

109:21-22 But You, O Lord, deal with me for Your name's sake; because Your mercy is good. Deliver me for I am poor and needy, and my heart is wounded within me.

109:26-27 Help me, O Lord my God! Oh, save me according to Your mercy, that they may know that this is Your hand—that You, Lord, have done it!

118:5-6 I called on You, Lord, in distress; Lord, You answered me and set me in a broad place. Lord, You are on my side; I will not fear. What can man do to me?

119:18 Open my eyes, that I may

see wondrous things from Your law.

119:25-26 My soul clings to the dust; I have declared my ways, and You answered me; teach me Your statutes. Revive me according to Your word.

119:124-125 Deal with Your servant according to Your mercy, and teach me Your statutes. I am Your servant; give me understanding, that I may know Your testimonies.

119:28 My soul melts from heaviness; strengthen me according to Your word.

119:32 I ask that You enlarge my heart?

119:153-156 Consider my affliction and deliver me, for I do not forget Your law. Plead my cause and redeem me; revive me according to Your word. Great are Your tender mercies, O Lord; revive me according to Your judgments.

120:1 In my distress I cried to You, Lord, and You heard me.

121:2-3 My help comes from You, Lord, who made heaven and earth. You will not allow my foot to be moved; You, who keeps me, will not slumber.

124:8 My help is in Your name Lord, who made heaven and earth.

126:5 I may sow in tears, but I shall reap in joy.

130:1-2 Out of the depths I have cried to You, O Lord, hear my voice! Let Your ears be attentive to the voice of my supplications.

140:4 Keep me, O Lord, from the hands of the wicked; preserve me from violent men, who have purposed to make my steps stumble.

140:6-8 I said to You, Lord: You are my God; hear the voice of my supplications, O Lord. O GOD, the strength of my salvation, You have covered my head in the day of battle. Do not grant, O Lord, the desires of the wicked; do not further their wicked scheme, lest they be exalted.

141:1-2 Lord, I cry out to You; make haste to me! Give ear to my voice when I cry out to You. Let my prayer be set before You as incense, the lifting up of my hands as the evening sacrifice.

141:8 But my eyes are upon You, O GOD, my Lord; in You I take refuge; do not leave my soul destitute.

142:1 I cry out to You, Lord, with my voice; with my voice to You, Lord, I make my supplication.

142:5-7 I cried out to You, O

Lord: I said, 'You are my refuge, My portion in the land of the living. Attend to my cry, for I am brought very low; deliver me from my persecutors, for they are stronger than I. Bring my soul out of prison, that I may praise Your name; the righteous shall surround me, for You shall deal bountifully with me.'

143:1 Hear my prayer, O Lord, Give ear to my supplications! In Your faithfulness answer me, and in Your righteousness.

143:3-4 For the enemy has persecuted my soul; You have crushed my life to the ground; You have made me dwell in darkness, like those who have long been dead. Therefore my spirit is overwhelmed within me; my heart within me is distressed.

143:7-11 Answer me speedily, O Lord; my spirit fails! Do not hide Your face from me, lest I be like those who go down into the pit. Cause me to hear Your lovingkindness in the morning, for in You do I trust; cause me to know the way in which I should walk, for I lift up my soul to You. Deliver me, O Lord, from my enemies; in You I take shelter. Teach me to do Your will, for You are my God; Your Spirit is good. Lead me in the land of uprightness.

143:11 Revive me, O Lord, for Your name's sake! For Your righteousness' sake bring my soul out of trouble.

144:7 Stretch out Your hand from above; rescue me and deliver me out of great waters.

Chapter 7

A.C.C.T.S.

119 ALPHABETIZED

A

37 Turn **away** my eyes from looking at worthless things, and revive me in Your way.

42 So shall I have an **answer** for him who reproaches me, or I trust in Your word.

65 You have dealt well with Your servant, O Lord, **according** to Your word.

67 Before I was **afflicted** I went **astray,** but now I keep Your word.

126 It is time for You to **act**, O Lord, for they have regarded Your law as void.

148 My eyes are **awake** through the night watches, that I may meditate on Your word.

161 Princes persecute me without a cause, but my heart stands in **awe** of Your word.

B

17 Deal **bountifully** with Your servant, that I may live and keep Your word.

72 The law of Your mouth is **better** to me than thousands of coins of gold and silver.

80 Let my heart be **blameless** regarding Your statutes, that I may not be ashamed.

C

6 Then I would not be ashamed, when I look into all Your **commandments.**

9 How can a young man **cleanse** his way? By taking heed according to Your word.

15 I will meditate on Your precepts, and **contemplate** Your ways.

31 I **cling** to Your testimonies; O Lord, do not put me to shame!

44 So shall I keep Your law **continually,** forever and ever.

63 I am a **companion** of all who fear You, and of those who keep Your precepts.

76 Let, I pray, Your merciful kindness be for my **comfort,** according to Your word to Your servant.

95 The wicked wait for me to destroy me, but I will **consider** Your

testimonies.

96 I have seen the *consummation* of all perfection, but Your *commandment* is exceedingly broad.

106 I have sworn and *confirmed* that I will keep Your righteous judgments.

109 My life is *continually* in my hand, yet I do not forget Your law.

128 Therefore all Your precepts concerning all things I *consider* to be right; I hate every false way.

D

4 You have commanded us to keep Your precepts *diligently.*

5 Oh, that my ways were *directed* to keep Your statutes!

24 Your testimonies also are my *delight* and my counselors.

26 I have *declared* my ways, and You answered me; teach me Your statutes.

35 Make me walk in the path of Your commandments, for I *delight* in it.

47 And I will *delight* myself in Your commandments, which I love.

70 Their heart is as fat as grease, but I *delight* in Your law.

92 Unless Your law had been my *delight,* I would then have perished in my affliction.

133 *Direct* my steps by Your word, and let no iniquity have dominion over me.

143 Trouble and anguish have overtaken me, yet Your commandments are my *delights.*

153 Consider my affliction and *deliver* me, for I do not forget Your law.

170 Let my supplication come before You; *deliver* me according to Your word.

174 I long for Your salvation, O Lord, and Your law is my *delight.*

E

32 I will run the course of Your commandments, for You shall *enlarge* my heart.

58 I *entreated* Your favor with my whole heart; be merciful to me according to Your word.

84 How many are the days of Your servant? When will You *execute* judgment on those who persecute me?

90 Your faithfulness *endures* to all generations; You *established* the earth, and it abides.

142 Your righteousness is an *everlasting* righteousness, and Your law is truth.

144 The righteousness of Your testimonies is *everlasting*; give me understanding, and I shall live.

160 The *entirety* of Your word is truth, and *every* one of Your righteous judgments *endures* forever.

F

16 I will delight myself in Your statutes; I will not *forget* Your word.

38 Establish Your word to Your servant, who is devoted to *fearing* You.

44 So shall I keep Your law continually; *forever* and ever.

61 The cords of the wicked have bound me, but I have not *forgotten* Your law.

73 Your hands have made me and *fashioned* me; give me understanding, that I may learn Your commandments.

75 I know, O Lord, that Your judgments are right, and that in *faithfulness* You have afflicted me.

79 Let those who *fear* You turn to me, those who know Your testimonies.

83 For I have become like a wineskin in smoke, yet I do not *forget* Your statutes.

86 All Your commandments are *faithful*; they persecute me wrongfully; help me!

89 *Forever*, O Lord, your word is settled in heaven.

152 Concerning Your testimonies, I have known of old that You have *founded* them *forever*.

G

29 Remove from me the way of lying, and *grant* me Your law graciously.

50 This is my comfort in my affliction, for Your word has *given* me life.

68 You are *good*, and do *good*; teach me Your statutes.

74 Those who fear You will be *glad* when they see me, because I have hoped in Your word.

130 The entrance of Your words *gives* light; it gives understanding to the simple.

H

2 Blessed are those who keep His testimonies, who seek Him with the whole *heart*!

11 Your word I have *hidden* in my *heart*, that I might not sin against You.

28 My soul melts from *heaviness*;

strengthen me according to Your word.

48 My *hands* also I will lift up to Your commandments, which I love, and I will meditate on Your statutes.

49 Remember the word to Your servant, upon which You have caused me to *hope.*

60 I made *haste*, and did not delay to keep Your commandments.

81 My soul faints for Your salvation, but I *hope* in Your word.

111 Your testimonies I have taken as a *heritage* forever, for they are the rejoicing of my *heart.*

114 You are my *hiding* place and my shield; I *hope* in Your word.

145 I cry out with my whole *heart*; *hear* me, O Lord! I will keep Your statutes.

147 I rise before the dawning of the morning, and cry for *help*; I *hope* in Your word.

166 Lord, I *hope* for Your salvation, and I do Your commandments.

173 Let Your *hand* become my *help*, for I have chosen Your precepts.

I

3 They also do no *iniquity*; they walk in His ways.

36 *Incline* my heart to Your testimonies, and not to covetousness.

53 *Indignation* has taken hold of me because of the wicked, who forsake Your law.

112 I have *inclined* my heart to perform Your statutes forever, to the very end.

J

30 I have chosen the way of truth; Your *judgments* I have laid before me.

39 Turn away my reproach, which I dread for Your *judgments* are good.

52 I remembered Your *judgments* of old, O Lord, and have comforted myself.

121 I have done *justice* and righteousness; do not leave me to my oppressors.

K

8 I will *keep* Your statutes; oh, do not forsake me utterly!

33 Teach me, O Lord, the way of Your statutes, and I shall *keep* it to the end.

66 Teach me good judgment and *knowledge*, for I believe Your commandments.

100 I understand more than the ancients, because I *keep* Your precepts.

115 Depart from me, you evildoers, for I will *keep* the commandments of my God!

125 I am Your servant; give me understanding, that I may *know* Your testimonies.

167 My soul *keeps* Your testimonies, and I love them exceedingly.

L

13 With my *lips* I have declared all the judgments of Your mouth.

20 My soul breaks with *longing* for Your judgments at all times.

45 And I will walk at *liberty*, for I seek Your precepts.

47 And I will delight myself in Your commandments, which I *love*.

55 I remember Your name in the night, O Lord, and I keep Your *law*.

71 It is good for me that I have been afflicted, that I may *learn* Your statutes.

88 Revive me according to Your *lovingkindness*, so that I may keep the testimony of Your mouth.

105 Your word is a *lamp* to my feet and a *light* to my path.

113 I hate the double-minded, but I *love* Your *law*.

127 Therefore I *love* Your commandments more than gold, yes, than fine gold!

M

15 I will *meditate* on Your precepts, and contemplate Your ways.

23 Princes also sit and speak against me, but Your servant *meditates* on Your statutes.

41 Let Your *mercies* come also to me, O Lord— Your salvation according to Your word.

48 My hands also I will lift up to Your commandments, which I love, and I will *meditate* on Your statutes.

64 The earth, O Lord, is full of Your *mercy*; teach me Your statutes.

76 Let, I pray, Your *merciful* kindness be for my comfort, according to Your word to Your servant.

77 Let Your tender *mercies* come to me, that I may live; for Your law is my delight.

78 Let the proud be ashamed, for they treated me wrongfully with falsehood; but I will *meditate* on Your precepts.

97 Oh, how I love Your law! It is my *meditation* all the day.

124 Deal with Your servant according to Your *mercy*, and teach me Your statutes.

132 Look upon me and be *merciful* to me, as Your custom is toward those who love Your name.

N

67 Before I was afflicted I went astray, but *now* I keep Your word.

85 The proud have dug pits for me, which is *not* according to Your law.

93 I will *never* forget Your precepts, for by them You have given me life.

102 I have *not* departed from Your judgments, for You Yourself have taught me.

110 The wicked have laid a snare for me, yet I have *not* strayed from Your precepts.

150 They draw *near* who follow after wickedness; they are far from Your law.

151 You are *near*, O Lord, and all Your commandments are truth.

O

34 Give me understanding, and I shall keep Your law; indeed, I shall *observe* it with my whole heart.

43 And take not the word of truth utterly *out* of my mouth, for I have hoped in Your ordinances.

91 They continue this day according to Your *ordinances*, for all are Your servants.

108 Accept, I pray, the freewill *offerings* of my mouth, O Lord, and teach me Your judgments.

117 Hold me up, and I shall be safe, and I shall *observe* Your statutes continually.

P

35 Make me walk in the *path* of Your commandments, for I delight in it.

40 Behold, I long for Your *precepts*; revive me in Your righteousness.

56 This has become mine, because I kept Your *precepts*.

57 You are my *portion*, O Lord; I have said that I would keep Your words.

69 The proud have forged a lie against me, but I will keep Your *precepts* with my whole heart.

87 They almost made an end of me on earth, but I did not forsake Your *precepts*.

131 I opened my mouth and *panted*, for I longed for Your

commandments.

141 I am small and despised, yet I do not forget Your *precepts.*140 Your word is very pure; therefore Your servant loves it.

154 *Plead* my cause and redeem me; revive me according to Your word.

164 Seven times a day I *praise* You, because of Your righteous judgments.

165 Great *peace* have those who love Your law, and nothing causes them to stumble.

175 Let my soul live, and it shall *praise* You; and let Your judgments help me.

R

14 I have *rejoiced* in the way of Your testimonies, as much as in all riches.

22 *Remove* from me reproach and contempt, for I have kept Your testimonies.

21 You *rebuke* the proud—the cursed, who stray from Your commandments.

25 My soul clings to the dust; *revive* me according to Your word.

32 I will run the course of Your commandments, for You shall enlarge my heart.

39 Turn away my *reproach*, which I dread, for Your judgments are good.

39 Turn away my *reproach*, which I dread, for Your judgments are good.

88 *Revive* me according to Your lovingkindness, so that I may keep the testimony of Your mouth.

101 I have *restrained* my feet from every evil way, that I may keep Your word.

107 I am afflicted very much; *revive* me, O Lord, according to Your word.

111 Your testimonies I have taken as a heritage forever, for they are the *rejoicing* of my heart.

118 You *reject* all those who stray from Your statutes, for their deceit is falsehood.

134 *Redeem* me from the oppression of man, that I may keep Your precepts.

154 Plead my cause and *redeem* me; revive me according to Your word.

156 Great are Your tender mercies, O Lord; *revive* me according to Your judgments.

162 I *rejoice* at Your word as one who finds great treasure.

S

19 I am a **stranger** in the earth; do not hide Your commandments from me.

23 Princes also **sit** and **speak** against me, but Your **servant** meditates on Your **statutes**.

41 Let Your mercies come also to me, O Lord — Your **salvation** according to Your word.

46 I will **speak** of Your testimonies also before kings, and will not be ashamed.

54 Your **statutes** have been my songs in the house of my pilgrimage.

82 My eyes fail from **searching** Your word, saying, "When will You comfort me?"

89 Forever, O Lord, Your word is **settled** in heaven.

94 I am Yours, **save** me; for I have sought Your precepts.

103 How **sweet** are Your words to my taste, **sweeter** than honey to my mouth!

106 I have **sworn** and confirmed that I will keep Your righteous judgments.

114 You are my hiding place and my **shield**; I hope in Your word.

122 Be surety for Your **servant** for good; do not let the proud oppress me.

123 My eyes fail from **seeking** Your **salvation** and Your righteous word.

135 Make Your face **shine** upon Your **servant**, and teach me Your statutes.

146 I cry out to You; **save** me, and I will keep Your testimonies.

155 **Salvation** is far from the wicked, for they do not **seek** Your **statutes**.

170 Let my **supplication** come before You; deliver me according to Your word.

176 I have gone astray like a lost sheep; seek Your **servant**, for I do not forget Your commandments.

T

12 Blessed are You, O Lord! **Teach** me Your statutes.

26 I have declared my ways, and You answered me; **teach** me Your statutes.

33 **Teach** me, O Lord, the way of Your statutes, and I shall keep it to the end.

59 I **thought** about my ways, and **turned** my feet to Your testimonies.

62 At midnight I will rise to give **thanks** to You, because of Your righteous judgments.

64 The earth, O Lord, is full of Your mercy; *teach* me Your statutes.

77 Let Your *tender* mercies come to me, that I may live; for Your law is my delight.

79 Let those who fear You *turn* to me, those who know Your *testimonies.*

119 You put away all the wicked of the earth like dross; therefore I love Your *testimonies.*

120 My flesh *trembles* for fear of You, and I am afraid of Your judgments.

124 Deal with Your servant according to Your mercy, and *teach* me Your statutes.

151 You are near, O Lord, and all Your commandments are *truth.*

162 I rejoice at Your word as one who finds great *treasure.*

156 Great are Your *tender* mercies, O Lord; revive me according to Your judgments.

157 Many are my persecutors and my enemies, yet I do not turn from Your *testimonies.*

172 My *tongue* shall speak of Your word, for all Your commandments are righteousness.

U

1 Blessed are the *undefiled* in the way, who walk in the law of the Lord!

7 I will praise You with *uprightness* of heart, when I learn Your righteous judgments.

43 And take not the word of truth *utterly* out of my mouth, for I have hoped in Your ordinances.

49 Remember the word to Your servant, *upon* which You have caused me to hope.

73 Your hands have made me and fashioned me; give me *understanding,* that I may learn Your commandments.

99 I have more *understanding* than all my teachers, for Your testimonies are my meditation.

104 Through Your precepts I get *understanding;* therefore I hate every false way.

116 *Uphold* me according to Your word, that I may live; and do not let me be ashamed of my hope.

125 I am Your servant; give me *understanding,* that I may know Your testimonies.

137 Righteous are You, O Lord, and *upright* are Your judgments.

169 Let my cry come before You, O Lord; give me *understanding* according to Your word.

171 My lips shall *utter* praise, for You teach me Your statutes.

are before You.

V

138 Your testimonies, which You have commanded, are righteous and *very* faithful.

149 Hear my *voice* according to Your lovingkindness; O Lord, revive me according to Your justice.

W

18 Open my eyes that I may see *wondrous* things from Your law.

10 With my *whole* heart I have sought You; oh, let me not *wander* from Your commandments!

18 Open my eyes that I may see *wondrous* things from Your law.

27 Make me understand the way of Your precepts; so shall I meditate on Your *wonderful* works.

37 Turn away my eyes from looking at *worthless* things, and revive me in Your *way*.

98 You, through Your commandments, make me *wiser* than my enemies; for they are ever with me.

129 Your testimonies are *wonderful*; therefore my soul keeps them.

168 I keep Your precepts and Your testimonies, for all my *ways*

Y

51 The proud have me in great derision, yet I do not turn aside from *Your* law.

72 The law of *Your* mouth is better to me than thousands of coins of gold and silver.

136 Rivers of water run down from my eyes, because men do not keep *Your* law.

158 I see the treacherous, and am disgusted, because they do not keep *Your* word.

159 Consider how I love *Your* precepts; revive me, O Lord, according to Your lovingkindness.

163 I hate and abhor lying, but I love *Your* law.

Z

139 My *zeal* has consumed me, because my enemies have forgotten Your words.

Chapter 8

A.C.C.T.S.

EXPRESSIONS OF WORSHIP

By Pastor Danny Hodges, Calvary Chapel, St. Petersburg, FL (calvarystp.org)

BOW DOWN – Job 1:20-21; Gen 24:12; 13; 26; 24:48; Ex 4:29-31; 12:26-27; 24:50-52; 34:5-8; 1 Chron. 29:20; Neh. 8:5; Job 1:20-21; Matt. 2:11

CLAP HANDS – Psalm 47:1; 28:2; 63:4

IN A BOAT – Matt 14:32

LEANING (canes, walkers, wheelchairs) – Hebrew 11:21

LIFT UP HOLY HANDS – Psalm 28:2; 63:4; 88:9; 119:48; 134:2; 141:2; 143:6; 1 Tim 2:8

LOOK UP – Psalm 123:1, 123:2, 121:1

ON YOUR FACE – Rev 11:16

SHOUT FOR JOY – Psalm 29; 35:26; 5:11; 20:4; 32:11; 33:3; 35:27; 47:1; 66:1; 71:23; 81:1; 95:1; 98:4, 98:6; 100:1; 108:9; Is.12:6; 24:14; 26:19; 35:2; Zech. 2:10; 9:9

SILENTLY – Mark 9:5; Rev 8:1

SIT – 2 Sam 7:18

STAND – Ex 33:11; Psalms 33:8

WITH MUSIC, DANCING AND A NEW SONG – Psalm 149:1; 149:5, 150:1-6

Chapter 9

A.C.C.T.S.

THE MASTER BUILDER

Every builder, architect and inventor creates things with a purpose. They plan things out, they test them and spend a lot of time designing them hoping to remove all the flaws. Some buildings are designed as one family dwellings, others were designed with the purpose of putting in business offices and others house art and history.

Each and every building was designed with a plan and a purpose. So my question to you is, just because you do not personally know the name of the architect that designed the Empire State Building, does that mean that he does not exist? You have never seen him or talked to him. You have never seen his face or even a picture of him. Does that mean he cannot possibly exist because you personally have not had a one on one relationship?

Just because you do not personally know the creator of the universe, does not mean that he doesn't exist. Things that are beyond someone's comprehension are easier to dismiss or considered fantasy. If you look at the most amazing designs ever made, and all of it's most intricate parts, it's pretty difficult to deny that there was an amazing builder and designer behind it. What is it?

Well, it's you, of course. I heard once that with the technology that we now have, we could create something equal to the human being. The designer would need to come up with a machine that could pump blood throughout the body 24/7 non-stop flawlessly for 70-80 years. It can not breakdown for even 5 minutes or the whole thing would collapse. It would have to equal all the systems in the human body, but we can now do it with our ever-growing superior knowledge and abilities. There is only one problem, while we are getting better and better with making things smaller and smaller we would still need an area the size of the state of Texas to house this one human that we inferior beings could create. Yikes!

But there is always a flip side to the coin. If we can create it, we can also destroy it. It takes months and sometimes years to build a house, a skyscraper or a bridge and only a day to completely demolish it. It is shocking, but those buildings are destroyed by choice. Some are destroyed by natural disasters like earthquakes. But it takes only a brief period of time to destroy what that designer and architect and construction workers took so long to build. That destroyer is a thief and comes with ill intentions.

So think about what God, the great creator, designer and architect did. When he created you and me, he had a purpose. We were designed with a specific plan and everyone has a different purpose. He said in John 10:10, *The thief comes only to steal and kill and destroy; I come that they may have life and have it to the full.*

Isn't it great to know that you were thought about before you were even born? You were designed with a purpose and a plan; you are not here randomly. It's not a mistake, you have a designer who thought about you long before you were even conceived. Sometimes that is a lot to take in, but it's true.

Jesus came to this world to give us a glimpse of who God is and His character. That God would stoop down to us when He is up there with all the best of everything and He decided to slum it, for us. John 3:16 *For God so loved the world that He gave his one and only Son, that whoever believes in Him, shall not perish but have eternal life.*

I don't know about you, but with all the sickness, sadness and destruction going on in this world today, I'm thankful that there is an escape. A way out of this mess because without the hope of a brighter future, what's the use of continuing on, even tomorrow? I could not keep going if I did not have the hope of something better coming.

Now, I'm going to bring a little bad news, but only for a short time. Man has a problem, and it is that we are going to die. We cannot avoid it no matter what we do. We need to deal with some reality of this fact.

God set a standard when he designed us, just like the architect and builder have a maintenance team. They check to make sure there are no cracks in the foundation. They do regular maintenance checks and are always doing little things to fix and repair. If they didn't, things would fall apart.

So God gave us a standard to live by to keep us safe, like a mother keeping her child from getting burned by the hot stove. She could let that child learn the hard way by ignoring the child reaching for the hot pan or she could say, "No, don't do that" Exodus 20 gives us a list of 10 things God said would hurt us if we do them. He said, don't do these things because they have consequences. He set a standard, just like our law enforcement today. Do not drink and drive. There is a severe penalty for it, if you are caught. And worse, you could die. Unfortunately, we didn't listen and we are paying a penalty. Romans 3:23 *For all have sinned and fall short of the glory of God.* We have missed the mark. We are not up to the standard. We have broken the law and are required to pay the penalty for it. Not one of us can live up to this list of only ten things. We have thousands of laws on the books in this country and we can't even keep up with ten.

The penalty for killing someone in most countries is death. That is the punishment God set for anyone who could not keep His ten commandments. Romans 6:23 *For the wages of sin is death, but the gift of God is eternal life in Christ Jesus our Lord.*

When you break the law there is a hearing, a judgment, sentencing then a punishment. Hebrews 9:27 *Just as man is destined to die once, and after that to face judgment.* We cannot think that when we die we can somehow escape this court hearing. There is no escape.

Well, our great designer and creator did not stop without finishing the plan. He sent us Jesus to fix the problem, those cracks in the foundation. He is the way to hold up that building that is starting to crumble. Jesus came to do what we cannot do in our own lifetime, in our own strength, in our own abilities. He lived that perfect life, upheld all ten of the laws and standards God set out. Then he did an amazing thing. He paid the penalty we were supposed to get.

We are the ones who committed the crimes and are supposed to be sentenced to death, but He took the punishment for us. He sacrificed His life in our place. 1 Peter 3:18 *For Christ died for sins once for all, the righteous for the unrighteous, to bring you to God. He was put to death in the body but made alive by the Spirit.*

Who are you willing to die for? Can you imagine saying to someone let me die for you? Would you serve the sentence for your neighbor? Maybe your child? Very rarely will anyone die for a righteous man, though for a good man someone might possibly dare to die. *But God demonstrates his own love for us in this: While we were still sinners, Christ died for us.* Romans 5:7-8 That is inconceivable, most of us cannot even begin to wrap our heads around this act of love.

A lot of people think they can earn their way into heaven. I hear people tell me, "I'm a good person, I don't hurt anyone." But did you ever tell a lie? Even a little, "white lie"? You just missed the mark. Did you ever take a pen or *post it* from work? That is stealing. You just missed the mark. You say, "Oh those are such minor things." But the law is the law and even though you thought you got away with it, someone is watching and someday you will have to pay the price.

Ephesians 2:8-9 *For it is by grace you have been saved, through faith – and this not from yourselves, it is the gift of God – not by works, so that no one can boast.* So that idea about getting into heaven because you are *basically a good person* is now out the window. That's not living up to God's standard and He judges based on those ten commandments, not that we tried to live a good life.

Well finally, I've got good news for you. Personally, I think this is GREAT news. You can live forever. I know, again, this is hard to comprehend, but remember, just because you can't see it with your eyes doesn't mean it doesn't exist. Just because you haven't seen the air you breath doesn't mean it doesn't exist. Just because you have never been to outer space and felt the effects of zero gravity, doesn't mean that it's not true.

There is a reward for believing in something you cannot see right this moment. John 1:12 *Yet to all who received him, to those who believed in his name, he gave the right to become children of God.* Aren't we all children of God? Well, there is one more step we need to take. It's called stepping off the cliff and trusting.

It requires us to do something to complete the process. You can tell someone you love them, but they won't walk down the aisle to the wedding alter unless both acknowledge the love is mutual.

Roman's 10:9-10 *If you confess with your mouth, 'Jesus is Lord,' and believe in your heart that God raised him from the dead, you will be saved. For it is with your heart that you believe and are justified and it is with your mouth that you confess and are saved.*

Now all this boils down to an amazing result. You can live your life for eternity. You don't ever have to worry about dieing. You don't have to worry what is on the other side of death. You don't have to fear that all the bad things in this world are all there is to offer. You don't have to worry about being sick, being sad, being lonely, being hurt by some bad person or being hit by a drunk driver. I could go on and on.

John 5:24 *I tell you the truth, whoever hears my word and believes him who sent me, has eternal life and will not be condemned; he has crossed over from death to life.*

The best thing is that as you have been learning about the character of God you can have that beautiful and wonderful one-on-one relationship with Him for all of eternity. If you have never given your heart to Jesus, you can do it any time or any place. Just pray this simple prayer:

Lord Jesus, I acknowledge that I have not lived up to your standard in my life. I realize that the penalty I am required to pay is more than I can bear. Lord, I acknowledge my sin and ask for your forgiveness. I thank you Jesus for taking the penalty that I deserve and giving me what you deserve, by dying on the cross for me and giving me life eternally. Thank you Jesus for dying in my place for me. Thank you for loving me that much. I now give my life back to you and ask that you would continue to show me how to live my life to please you and to know you better. In Jesus name, Amen.

You now have the assurance of eternal life. Life in abundance. You next step is to find a church that will teach you how to live this new life. Read the Bible but always invite the Holy Spirit to teach you. The Holy Spirit will open your eyes like never before, you will hear and understand things that you cannot imagine. The Bible is the only book that you can interact with the author as you read it. If you don't understand something ask Him. But always invite Him before you start reading. Ask for wisdom and understanding and for a change of heart.

God bless you and keep you until He returns to take his children home for eternity. I'll see you there.

A.C.C.T.S. of Prayer in the Psalms

Date	Prayer Request	Answered

Date	Prayer Request	Answered

WORDS & VERSES TO REMEMBER

_____   _____
_____   _____
_____   _____
_____   _____
_____   _____
_____   _____
_____   _____
_____   _____
_____   _____
_____   _____
_____   _____
_____   _____
_____   _____
_____   _____
_____   _____
_____   _____
_____   _____
_____   _____
_____   _____
_____   _____
_____   _____
_____   _____

OTHER BOOKS BY JOSIPHINE LONGO
Available Soon:
CHASING AFTER GOD'S HEART
This is an in depth look at the words that describe God. Use this
workbook as a companion to the **A.C.C.T.S. of Prayer in the Psalms** book.

THE WISDOM OF KING SOLOMON IN THE PROVERBS & ECCLESASTIES
A reference book on the wisdom of King Solomon by topics with the
related scripture reference.

FAITH, HOPE, LOVE, TRUST & FORGIVENESS IN THE WORD
You can rest, assured that we can trust in God who sent Jesus to rescue
us from this world. This is proof at your finger tips from the word, on
how to keep the faith, hope & trust in the Lord until He returns.

See inside front cover for information on ordering books. or visit: www.tididi.com

LaVergne, TN USA
09 October 2009
160408LV00002B/3/P